LUKE

The Gospel of the Son of Man

LUKE
The Gospel of the Son of Man

by

PAUL N. BENWARE

MOODY PRESS
CHICAGO

Library of Congress Cataloging in Publication Data

Benware, Paul N., 1942-
Luke, the gospel of the son of man.

(Everyman's Bible commentary)
Bibliography: p.
Includes index.
1. Bible. N.T. Luke—Criticism, interpretation, etc.
2. Son of Man—Biblical teaching. I. Title. II. Series.
BS2595.2.B46 1985 226'.407 85-4860
ISBN 0-8024-2074-5 (pbk.)

3 4 5 6 7 Printing/EP/90 89

Printed in the United States of America

CONTENTS

INTRODUCTION AND BACKGROUND TO LUKE

The Author

From earliest times the church has held that Luke wrote the third gospel, even though his name is not mentioned in the gospel itself. Almost all are in agreement that the author of the third gospel is the same one who penned the book of Acts. Both books are dedicated to Theophilus, both are similar in language and style, and the latter refers to the former.[1] It is also clear that the writer of these two books was a companion of the apostle Paul, as the "we" sections of Acts indicate (Acts 16:10, 11; 20:5; 21:1). In these sections of Acts, the author includes himself in the journeys of Paul. The question then becomes one of identifying the right companion of Paul. Luke was a close companion of Paul (Col. 4:12-14; 2 Tim. 4:11; Phile. 24). After viewing all of Paul's known companions and after noting all the historical data, it appears Luke best fits the scriptural information.[2]

Tradition also affirms the author to be Luke. There is a unanimous testimony from the early church Fathers that Luke, who was from Antioch of Syria, wrote the third gospel. Irenaeus (about A.D. 185), Justin Martyr (about A.D. 150), the Muratorian Canon (about A.D. 195), the anti-Marcionite Prologue to the third gospel (about A.D. 160), and a number of

1. Norval Geldenhuys, *Commentary on the Gospel of Luke* (Grand Rapids: Eerdmans, 1966), p. 15.
2. Leon Morris, *The Gospel According to St. Luke* (Grand Rapids: Eerdmans, 1982), pp. 16-17.

other sources agree that the author of the third gospel was Luke.[3]

Medical language points to Luke the physician as being the author.[4] Being a physician, Luke was well educated and thus capable of writing in the good Greek style of Acts and the third gospel. Some have suggested that since Luke was from Antioch of Syria, he probably would have gone to the closest university for his training, and that was at Tarsus. It is further suggested that Luke came to a knowledge of the Savior while there, being influenced by another young intellectual from Tarsus, one by the name of Saul.[5] This, of course, is speculation, though it is possible.

Luke was a close friend and companion of the apostle Paul. Luke joined Paul at Troas on Paul's second missionary journey. On that journey, Luke evidently stayed at Philippi (Acts 16) and was a key to the ministry of that new church. Paul continued on his journey but returned to Philippi some six years later on his third missionary trip. Luke rejoined him at that point and journeyed on to Palestine. During that six-year period at Philippi, Luke not only ministered to the church there but evidently was Paul's representative in Macedonia. Some believe that Luke is the "brother" noted for his excellence in the gospel ministry in that area (2 Cor. 8:18).[6] Luke remained with Paul for the two years of Paul's imprisonment at Caesarea and then accompanied him to Rome (Acts 28).

Luke himself was a Gentile, as the context of Colossians 4 would indicate (Luke not being included in the list of the "circumcision"). Luke is therefore the only Gentile writer of Scripture. The books of Luke and Acts account for 25 percent of the New Testament.

3. Geldenhuys, pp. 17-18.
4. Alfred Plummer, *A Critical and Exegetical Commentary on the Gospel According to St. Luke,* 3d ed. (Edinburgh: T. and T. Clark, 1900), p. lvix.,
5. W. Graham Scroggie, *A Guide to the Gospels* (Old Tappan, N. J.: Revell, 1962), p. 335.
6. Merrill C. Tenney, *New Testament Survey,* rev. ed. (Grand Rapids: Eerdmans, 1967), p. 173.

The Place and Date of Writing

Unlike most of the books in the New Testament, the date of Luke is difficult to determine. Over the years a number of possibilities have been suggested. Of these, two are seen as most probable. One is that Luke was written around A.D. 58 from the city of Caesarea while Paul was imprisoned there. A second possibility is that it was written from Rome shortly before A.D. 65. This second position is probably better, though either date is acceptable.

The Purpose of Luke

In the introduction to his gospel, Luke explained his purpose for writing. He wrote to present a historically accurate and chronologically correct account of the life and ministry of Jesus Christ. He wanted his readers to be well grounded in their faith.

The Theme of Luke

The four gospels are not biographies of the life of Christ, for the simple reason that almost thirty years of His life are really not dealt with. The four gospels view Jesus Christ from four different vantage points. Luke views Jesus Christ as a man, a real human being. Jesus Christ was the perfect man, as well as being God (John), the great King (Matthew), and the obedient Servant of the Lord (Mark). Luke uses the phrase "Son of Man" twenty-four times in his gospel. This title is the one that Jesus used most frequently of Himself. The phrase "Son of Man" emphasizes His humanity, and Jesus used it especially when referring to His sufferings and death. It is also clear that Jesus used the expression because of its important connection with Daniel 7:13, where the phrase is obviously messianic. This was a phrase, therefore, that emphasized both His humanity and His messiahship.[7]

Luke seems to have a special audience in mind as he writes,

7. Geldenhuys, p. 352.

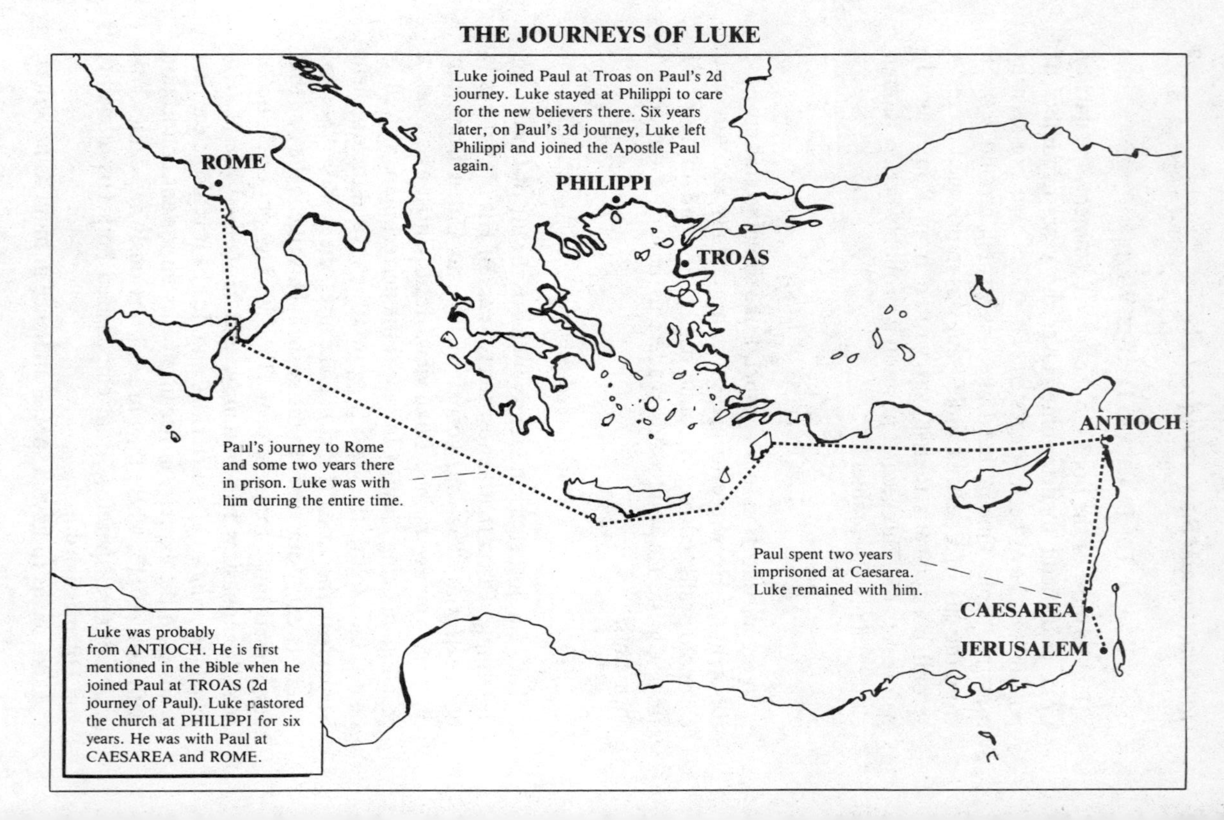
THE JOURNEYS OF LUKE
Luke joined Paul at Troas on Paul's 2d journey. Luke stayed at Philippi to care for the new believers there. Six years later, on Paul's 3d journey, Luke left Philippi and joined the Apostle Paul again.
ROME
PHILIPPI
TROAS
ANTIOCH
Paul's journey to Rome and some two years there in prison. Luke was with him during the entire time.
Paul spent two years imprisoned at Caesarea. Luke remained with him.
CAESAREA
JERUSALEM
Luke was probably from ANTIOCH. He is first mentioned in the Bible when he joined Paul at TROAS (2d journey of Paul). Luke pastored the church at PHILIPPI for six years. He was with Paul at CAESAREA and ROME.

Fig. I.1

namely the Greek. Luke's approach and view of Christ would appeal to the Greek, who was constantly looking for the ideal man. Luke presents and describes the sinless, perfect "Son of Man."

Luke's gospel brings out the wider implications of the gospel of Jesus Christ. Salvation is not just for the Jew, but it is also for the Gentile. For example, the message of the angels is directed to all men (2:14), old Simeon foretells Jesus' being a light to the Gentiles (2:32), and Luke goes further in giving the quote from Isaiah that "all flesh shall see the salvation of God" (3:6).

Luke's Unique Contribution

Each of the four gospels has unique features as each tells its story of the life of Jesus Christ. Over 50 percent of Luke's gospel is unique, containing materials found nowhere else. Without Luke, certain periods of Christ's life and ministry would be unknown to us. Luke alone gives certain important chronological notations (2:1; 3:2; 3:23). Luke has a greater focus on individuals than do the other gospels. For example, Luke mentions thirteen women not found in the other gospels. It can also be said that Luke's gospel has a more comprehensive range than the others. It begins with the announcements concerning the births of John the Baptist and Jesus and ends with a reference to the ascension of Christ.

It is impossible to say how many miracles Jesus Christ performed during His ministry, because many are referred to collectively. There are about a dozen passages in the gospels where miracles are summarized for us. There are thirty-five miracles specifically detailed in the gospels, twenty of which are found in Luke. Of the twenty in Luke, seven are unique to this gospel alone.[8]

1. The miraculous catch of fish, 5:1-11
2. The raising of the widow's son, 7:11-17

8. Scroggie, *A Guide to the Gospels,* pp. 349-53.

3. The casting out of a demon, 11:14
4. The healing of a crippled woman, 13:10-17
5. The healing of a man with dropsy, 14:1-4
6. The healing of the ten lepers, 17:11-19
7. The restoring of Malchus's ear, 22:49-51

The teachings of Jesus were full of illustrations from life. Many of Christ's illustrations could be classified as parables. But of those that are extended narratives, there are some fifty-one "parables" spoken by Christ. Needless to say, this number is not fixed, since there is much disagreement as to what constitutes a parable. However, of the fifty-one so classified, thirty-five are found in Luke, and nineteen of those are unique to this gospel.

1. The two debtors, 7:41
2. The good Samaritan, 10:30
3. The friend at midnight, 11:5
4. The rich fool, 12:13
5. The watching servants, 12:35
6. The faithful steward, 12:41
7. The barren fig tree, 13:6
8. The chief seats, 14:7
9. The great supper, 14:16
10. The unfinished tower, 14:28
11. The unwaged war, 14:31
12. The lost coin, 15:8
13. The prodigal son, 15:11
14. The unfaithful steward, 16:1
15. The rich man and Lazarus (?), 16:19
16. The unprofitable servants, 17:7
17. The unrighteous judge, 18:1
18. The Pharisee and the publican, 18:9
19. The pounds, 19:11

Some occurrences in Christ's life and some of His recorded teachings are very similar. Sometimes it is clear that, although they are similar, they took place at different times or locations. Listed below is a group of events that are not in the category of parables or miracles but are incidents recorded only by Luke.

1. The announcements of the births of John and Jesus, 1:5-56
2. The accounts of the births of John and Jesus, 1:57-2:20
3. The events in the Temple at Jesus' presentation, 2:21-38
4. The story of Jesus at age twelve, 2:39-52
5. The dating of the start of John's ministry, 3:1-2
6. The impact of John's ministry, 3:10-15
7. The genealogy of Jesus, 3:23-38
8. Christ's rejection at the Nazareth synagogue, 4:15-30
9. The anointing of Jesus in the house of Simon, 7:36-50
10. The women who ministered to Christ, 8:1-3
11. James and John desiring to call down fire, 9:51-56
12. The sending out of the seventy, 10:1-12
13. The return and the reporting of the seventy, 10:17-24
14. Christ at the home of Martha and Mary, 10:38-42
15. Christ entertained by a Pharisee, 11:37-54
16. Discourse to a large crowd, 12:1-53
17. Pilate's murder of Galileans, 13:1-5
18. Teaching on the number to be saved, 13:22-30
19. Teaching on discipleship, 14:25-35
20. Questions about the kingdom, 17:20-37
21. Conversation with Zacchaeus, 19:1-10
22. Christ's warning to the disciples, 22:31-38
23. Events in Gethsemane, 22:43-44
24. Trial before Herod, 23:6-12
25. Christ's words to the women of Jerusalem, 23:27-31
26. The repentent thief, 23:39-43
27. Appearance to the Emmaus disciples, 24:13-35
28. Details of His appearance to the eleven, 24:37-49
29. Christ's ascension, 24:50-53

Outline

The Prologue of Luke's Gospel, 1:1-4

I. The Coming of Jesus the Son of Man, 1:5—4:13
   A. His Entrance into the World, 1:5—2:52
      1. The announcement of the birth of John the Baptist, 1:5-25
      2. The announcement of the birth of Jesus, 1:26-38
      3. The journey of Mary to the home of Elizabeth, 1:39-56
      4. The birth of John the Baptist, 1:57-80
      5. The birth of Jesus, 2:1-52
   B. His Presentation to Israel, 3:1—4:13
      1. The forerunner of Jesus, 3:1-20
      2. The baptism of Jesus, 3:21-22
      3. The genealogy of Jesus, 3:23-38
      4. The testing of Jesus, 4:1-13

II. The Ministry of Jesus the Son of Man, 4:14—9:50
   A. His Ministry Begins, 4:14-30
   B. His Authority Demonstrated, 4:31—6:11
      1. His authority over demons, 4:31-37
      2. His authority over sickness and disease, 4:38-44
      3. His authority over nature, 5:1-11
      4. His authority over leprosy, 5:12-26
      5. His authority over men, 5:27-29
      6. His authority over men's traditions, 5:30-39
      7. His authority over the sabbath, 6:1-11
   C. His Disciples Chosen, 6:12-49
   D. His Multifaceted Ministry, 7:1—9:50
      1. His ministry to a Roman centurion, 7:1-10
      2. His ministry to a grieving widow, 7:11-17
      3. His ministry to a doubting prophet, 7:18-35
      4. His ministry to a repentant prostitute, 7:36-50
      5. His ministry supported, 8:1-3
      6. His ministry of teaching, 8:4-21
      7. His ministry to the fearful disciples, 8:22-25

8. His ministry to the demon-possessed, 8:26-39
9. His ministry to the great and lowly, 8:40-56
10. His ministry through His disciples, 9:1-9
11. His ministry to the hungry, 9:10-17
12. His ministry of revelation, 9:18-50

III. The Ministry of Jesus the Son of Man in Times of Rejection, 9:51—19:27
   A. His Final Journey to Jerusalem, 9:51-62
      1. The rejection by the Samaritans, 9:51-56
      2. The responses of potential disciples, 9:57-62
   B. His Instruction in View of His Rejection, 10:1—19:27
      1. The sending out of the seventy to minister, 10:1-24
      2. The parable of the Good Samaritan, 10:25-37
      3. Mary and Martha, worship and service, 10:38-42
      4. Instruction on prayer, 11:1-13
      5. The rejection of Jesus by the leaders of Israel, 11:14-54
      6. Instruction concerning hypocrisy, 12:1-12
      7. Instruction concerning covetousness, 12:13-34
      8. Instruction concerning watchfulness, 12:35-41
      9. Instruction concerning faithfulness, 12:42-48
      10. Instruction concerning the effect of His coming, 12:49-53
      11. Instruction concerning the signs of the times, 12:54-59
      12. Instruction concerning repentance, 13:1-9
      13. Instruction concerning Israel's need, 13:10-17
      14. Instruction concerning the kingdom program, 13:18-21
      15. Instruction while traveling toward Jerusalem, 13:22-30
      16. Instruction concerning Jerusalem, 13:31-35
      17. Instruction in the house of a Pharisee, 14:1-24

18. Instruction concerning discipleship, 14:25-35
19. Instruction concerning God's attitude toward sinners, 15:1-32
20. Instruction concerning wealth, 16:1-31
21. Instruction concerning forgiveness, 17:1-6
22. Instruction concerning service, 17:7-10
23. Instruction concerning thankfulness, 17:11-19
24. Instruction concerning the second coming, 17:20—18:8
25. Instruction concerning self-righteousness, 18:9-14
26. Instruction concerning entrance into the kingdom, 18:15-30
27. Instruction concerning His death, 18:31-34
28. Ministry to the blind man at Jericho, 18:35-43
29. Ministry to Zacchaeus, 19:1-10
30. Instruction concerning the delayed kingdom, 19:11-27

IV. The Suffering and Sacrifice of Jesus the Son of Man, 19:28—23:56
- A. His Triumphal Entry, 19:28-44
- B. His Cleansing of the Temple, 19:45-48
- C. His Debates with the Leaders, 20:1—21:38
    1. The question of authority, 20:1-19
    2. The question of paying taxes, 20:20-26
    3. The question about resurrection, 20:27-40
    4. The question about Messiah's lineage, 20:41-44
    5. The denunciation of the religious leaders, 20:45-47
    6. Jesus' observation about giving, 21:1-4
    7. Jesus' prophetic discourse, 21:5-38
- D. His Betrayal and Arrest, 22:1-54
    1. The betrayal by Judas Iscariot, 22:1-6
    2. The last supper of Jesus and the disciples, 22:7-38
    3. The agony of Jesus in Gethsemane, 22:39-46
    4. The arrest of Jesus in Gethsemane, 22:47-53

- E. His Trials, 22:54—23:25
    1. His trials before the Jews, 22:54-71
    2. His trials before the Romans, 23:1-25
- F. His Death, 23:26-56
    1. On the way to the Crucifixion, 23:26-32
    2. The crucifixion of Jesus, 23:33-49
    3. The burial of Jesus, 23:50-56

V. The Final Authentication of Jesus the Son of Man, 24:1-53
- A. His empty tomb, 24:1-12
- B. His Emmaus disciples, 24:13-35
- C. His resurrection appearances, 24:36-49
- D. His ascension into heaven, 24:50-53

The Synoptic Problem

Luke, Matthew, and Mark are commonly referred to as the "synoptic gospels." *Synoptic* is a Greek word that means a "seeing together." This term emphasizes the fact that Matthew, Mark, and Luke basically have a common viewpoint of the life and ministry of Christ. John's gospel is not part of this group because over 90 percent of that gospel contains unique material.

The *Synoptic Problem* is the phrase used to describe the difficulty that scholars have in dealing with the apparent interrelationship of Matthew, Mark, and Luke. Scholars have pointed out that not only do the synoptic gospels have the same general historical structure, but they often have certain clear verbal agreements. The similarities are so numerous and with such obvious verbal agreement that it cannot be coincidental. Many conclude there was literary dependence among Matthew, Mark, and Luke.[9] But exactly which writer depended on which other writers? And how does one account for the striking differences in their accounts? The answers to these and other related questions have occupied the attention of New Testa-

9. Everett F. Harrison, *Introduction to the New Testament* (Grand Rapids: Eerdmans, 1968), pp. 136-53.

ment scholars. Several basic solutions have been set forth. One theory is that of oral tradition. This postulates that as the apostles and leaders of the early church preached about the works and the teachings of Christ, their preaching tended toward a fixed form. The accounts and stories were passed on relatively unchanged from person to person. Thus by the time they were written down, a basic, fixed form had been achieved, and that accounts for the similarities. Although there may be some validity to the idea of oral tradition, it does not account for the differences in the gospel narratives, and it does not adequately deal with the difficulty of a church's spreading out of the apostles' influence.

A second theory, the Two Document Hypothesis, has gained wide acceptance in modern times. This theory sets forth the idea that Mark was the first gospel written and that Matthew and Luke based their gospels on Mark. Furthermore, Matthew and Luke also used a second document, called "Q" (from the German *quelle,* meaning "source"). This source document "Q" is alleged to account for numerous similarities between Matthew and Luke in places where the two differ from Mark. The arguments surrounding this theory are many and complex. However, certain significant problems exist.

First, there is such a heavy emphasis on the use of written documents in this theory, and other similar ones, that the personal relationships and contacts of the gospel writers are not properly emphasized. Matthew was an eyewitness of those things that he wrote about (which raises the question as to why Matthew should depend on Mark, who was not present when these events occurred). Mark was closely associated with the apostles. Luke, during the two years of Paul's Caesarean imprisonment, stayed in Palestine with the apostles. His contacts were undoubtedly numerous; perhaps he had direct contact with Matthew and Mark. It must be remembered that these three gospel writers were not penning their gospels in isolation far from Palestine and the people who had surrounded Christ in His earthly life and ministry.

Another problem with the widely accepted Two Document Hypothesis is its basis on the hypothetical document "Q".

There is no copy of such a document and great question as to whether or not such a document ever existed. Yet another difficulty with the theory is the priority of Mark. The uniform tradition of the church from very ancient times has been the priority of Matthew. This ancient tradition clearly has Matthew writing the first gospel. The more recent documentary theory of the nineteenth century has no evidence that the ancient view is in error.[10]

Perhaps Luke himself has the key to the solution of the Synoptic Problem. In the prologue to his gospel (Luke 1:1-4), he explains how his gospel came into existence. It is quite clear that he did not simply copy someone else's work, editing here and there. Luke did indeed use some written records, which he carefully checked for accuracy. Unlike Matthew and to some degree Mark, Luke was not an eyewitness of the events pertaining to Christ's life. But he did speak with those who were eyewitnesses.

Luke also mentions the "ministers of the word." These may have been individuals in the early church who had a special function as tradition-bearers, passing on in a fairly set form truths about Christ. There were evidently sayings of Christ that were passed on from person to person in a fixed form (as in Acts 20:35). Luke used many sources and spoke with many people in writing his gospel. And much the same was probably true of Matthew and Mark. In all of this, the foundational role of the Holy Spirit must be remembered. One of the Spirit's ministries was to guide men into the truth and enable them to recall, without distortion or error, the truth about Christ (John 14:26; 16:14-15; 1 Cor. 2:12). This He did. Nineteen centuries have gone by since the gospels were written, with the result that many of the facts about their writing are not clear. It is quite clear, however, that what they wrote is accurate, without error, directed by the Holy Spirit, and therefore authoritative in our lives.[11]

10. Robert L. Thomas and Stanley N. Gundry, *A Harmony of the Gospels* (Chicago: Moody, 1978), pp. 276-77.
11. Ibid., pp. 278-79.

An Overview of the Life of Christ

Some understanding of an overview of Christ's life and ministry is needed before there can be an appreciation of the details of the gospel. The accounts of Christ's birth, death, and resurrection, the story of the feeding of the 5,000, the parable of the Good Samaritan, and numerous other portions are quite familiar to most Christians. But often there is little understanding of the relationships that exist between these events, miracles, and teachings. There is a pattern to the life and ministry of Christ. When the pattern is seen, the specific accounts in the gospels become clearer.

The life of Christ can be separated into eight main divisions. Although the gospel accounts themselves are not divided in such a way, this nevertheless is a way to organize the great mass of material given in the gospel records (see fig. I.2).

THE BIRTH AND CHILDHOOD OF JESUS CHRIST

Breaking the silence of four centuries, the angel Gabriel came announcing the births of John the Baptist and Jesus. In fulfillment of the prophets Isaiah and Malachi, John the Baptist, the forerunner of Jesus Christ, was born. Micah and Isaiah prophesied of the birth of the God-man and the location of that birth in Bethlehem (Isa. 9:6; Mic. 5:2). Our knowledge of this first period of Christ's life is limited, even though the period covers about thirty years. After His birth at Bethlehem, Jesus, along with Joseph and Mary, fled to Egypt. Following a short period there, the family was directed by God to return to Palestine and settle in the Galilean town of Nazareth. Here Jesus learned the carpentry trade from Joseph. Jesus evidently lived a normal life during the years of His youth. Joseph probably died during the years of Jesus' early manhood, placing Jesus in the position of responsibility for the family. Luke's gospel gives most of our information about this period of Christ's life.

PREPARATION FOR THE MINISTRY OF CHRIST

It was not until He was about thirty years of age that His purpose of coming to this world was formally announced to

Fig. I.2

AN OVERVIEW OF THE LIFE OF CHRIST

	1	2	3	4	5	6	7	8
PERIOD IN THE LIFE OF CHRIST	Birth and Childhood of Christ	Preparation for Christ's Ministry	Early Ministry of Christ	Great Galilean Ministry of Christ	Special Training of the Twelve	Later Judean Ministry of Christ	Later Perean Ministry of Christ	The Last Days in Jerusalem
PRIMARY GOSPELS	Matthew and Luke	Matthew Mark Luke John	John	Matthew and Mark	Matthew and Mark	Luke and John	Luke	Matthew Mark Luke John
CHAPTERS IN LUKE	1:1—2:52	3:1—4:13	—	4:14—8:22	8:22—9:50	9:51—13:21	13:22—19:28	20:1—24:53
YEARS IN CHRIST'S LIFE	About 30 years		Approximately 3½ years					

the nation of Israel. John the Baptist, who was six months older than Jesus, prepared the way by proclaiming the presence of the long awaited Messiah, the Savior. John prepared the nation by preaching a message of repentance with water baptism as a visible sign of that repentance. Those who repented and were baptized were thus identified with the Messiah. The Lord Jesus Himself was prepared for His public ministry through His baptism and temptation. His baptism was His anointing into the office of king, and His temptation revealed His sinless character.

THE EARLY MINISTRY OF CHRIST

Jesus began His ministry in the same area in which He had been baptized, the region around the Jordan River. His first concern was to surround Himself with men who could help Him establish His much-prophesied and long-awaited earthly kingdom. His first followers were men who had been disciples of John the Baptist. His early ministry lasted for about one year, and Jesus moved about to all places in Palestine where potential believers might be found. He began working miracles designed to awaken the people to the fact that Messiah had indeed come. He worked His first miracle at Cana of Galilee, where He changed the water into wine (John 2). His famous discussions with the religious leader Nicodemus and the sinful Samaritan woman at the well took place during this time period also (John 3-4). His first cleansing of the Temple occurred in the early ministry as well. This event alerted the religious leaders to His presence (John 2). Luke and the other synoptic gospels give no information about this period. (See map, fig. I.3, for locations mentioned in this overview.)

THE GREAT GALILEAN MINISTRY

When John the Baptist was jailed by wicked Herod Antipas, Jesus went to Galilee and made Capernaum the base for His next year of ministry. Jesus and His disciples went throughout this region preaching the good news about the kingdom and working many miracles. The Lord Jesus' popularity reached its

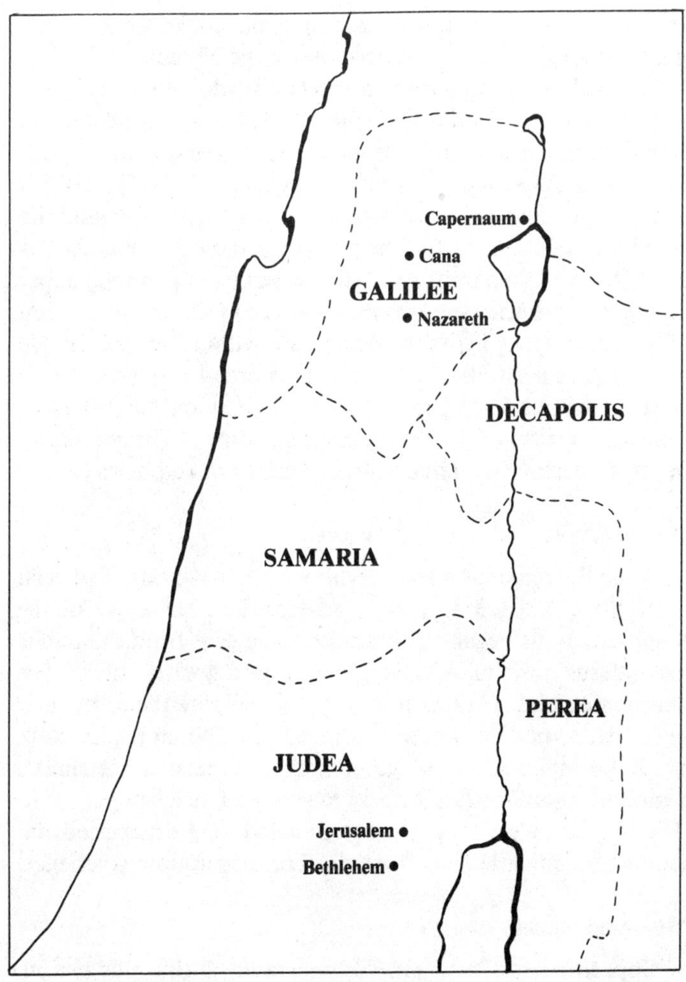

Fig. I.3

peak during this period of His ministry. The feeding of the 5,000 men at the very end of this period indicated how popular He had become with the common people of Galilee. He was viewed as a prophet of God, but the vast majority did not see Him as "the Christ, the Son of the Living God." He did some of His greatest works during this time and spoke some of His greatest words, such as the Sermon on the Mount.

But as Jesus' popularity increased, so did the opposition from the religious leaders of Israel. A crisis was reached in this period when these religious leaders formally and publicly concluded that Jesus was from the devil and not from God. With this terrible and official rejection of their King and His kingdom, the ministry of Christ made a radical change. Jesus began to speak in parables in order to veil truth from the unbelievers. His miracles were no longer given as signs to the nation of Israel, only as helps to individuals within the nation. He began to speak of His death and the church for the first time. And the emphasis of His ministry was now on His believing followers instead of the nation at large. Some of His popularity began to decline as opinion about Him became polarized.

THE SPECIAL TRAINING OF THE TWELVE

When the religious leaders, who were in positions of official authority (Matt. 23:2-3), rejected Him and His offer of the kingdom, Jesus began to withdraw somewhat from the public view. Jesus now turned His attention in a greater way to His chosen disciples. He was now going to prepare them for their new role, as part of the foundation of the church (Eph. 2:20). Since the King and His kingdom had been rejected, the church would be established, and these men would be a key part of it. The disciples were taught many things during this period, including the great lessons from the Transfiguration experience.

THE LATER JUDEAN MINISTRY

Opposition to Christ steadily increased during this period, and if the opportunity had presented itself, the Jewish leaders would have killed Him. But, as John states, His "hour had not yet come." The events recorded in this period are primarily extended accounts of single days, during which the Lord debated the leaders of Israel. Teaching His followers was still of paramount importance during this time.

THE LATER PEREAN MINISTRY

Approximately three or four months before His crucifixion, Jesus withdrew across the Jordan River into the area of Perea. He did return into Judea during this period, but the time was primarily spent in Perea (John 10:40). Both the crowds and the opposition to Him were great. The great division of attitude about Jesus was seen when Lazarus was raised from the dead. Many believed, but others wanted to put Lazarus to death. Many of Jesus' parables were spoken during this period, as He desired to communicate truth to believers while concealing the truth from unbelievers.

THE LAST DAYS IN JERUSALEM

Approximately 25 percent of the gospel records deals with this final and crucial period of time. The climax of the opposition against Christ reached its peak during the week of the Passover feast. The diabolical hatred of Jesus by the religious leaders was again and again revealed. Jesus answered all of their devious questions with great wisdom and discernment, yet they still wanted to destroy Him. Jesus gave His followers more important information in such teachings as the Upper Room discourse and the Olivet discourse. The gospel writers give us a glimpse of many events in those significant hours before the crucifixion, as Jesus went to the Garden of Gethsemane and prayed, was arrested, faced the trials of Jews and Romans, and was condemned to die. They recorded the most important single event in the history of mankind, the sacrificial death of the Son of Man. This they followed with the accounts of the glorious triumph of the Son of Man over Satan, sin, and death as He was raised from the dead. New life is now offered to mankind, and that is the "good news" that the gospel writers communicate to us.

1

THE COMING OF JESUS THE SON OF MAN

(LUKE 1:1—4:13)

The Prologue of Luke's Gospel (1:1-4)

Following the customary approach of classical historians, Luke prefaced his gospel by declaring his purpose for writing and the sources used in his writing. His preface (1:1-4) is actually just one sentence in the Greek, revealing that Luke was quite capable of writing in the classical Greek style.

The gospel is directed to a man by the name of Theophilus (which means "lover of God" or "dear to God"). The term "most excellent Theophilus" (1:3) suggests that this Gentile friend of Luke was a man of high official position.

Luke's purpose in writing was to give to Theophilus (and all the readers of this gospel) the assurance that the faith he had embraced rested on a sure and solid historical foundation. After doing a thorough study of the matter, Luke stated that it was his intention to systematize his presentation. The phrase "in consecutive order" (1:3) suggests that Luke's presentation would be done in a logical way, with the probability that the gospel would reveal an accurate chronological order as well.

Luke apparently used three sources in gathering material for his gospel. First, he studied the many written documents that were available (1:1). No doubt many of the apostles and disciples had written down accounts of Christ's teachings and His miracles in order to share them with friends, new converts, and potential converts. These documents were available to Luke, and he studied them carefully. Second, Luke spoke with eyewitnesses of Christ's ministry (1:2). As Luke interviewed these people, he was able to pick up information that would not be found in writing. For example, much of Luke's birth narrative could well have come to Luke from Mary herself. Third, Luke spoke of the "servants of the Word" (1:2). Many Bible scholars believe that these individuals had a special function as tradition-bearers; that is, they passed on in a fixed form truths about Christ. It is believed that these individuals, with the approval of the apostles, had a significant ministry in relating these truths during a time before the inspired gospels were written.

Luke, therefore, used a variety of means in acquiring material for his gospel. Luke's research and study does not in any way lessen the concept of inspiration for his gospel. Luke studied carefully the material that he gathered, but still it was the Holy Spirit who guided him and kept him from error. The truth of the inspiration of the Scriptures has to do with the actual written word and not with the way in which the author obtained his message. Luke's gospel is just as inspired as the Ten Commandments or the book of Romans.

I. The Coming of Jesus the Son of Man (1:5—4:13)

A. His entrance into the world (1:5—2:52)

1. The announcement of the birth of John the Baptist (1:5-25). Bible scholars often refer to the period between the Old and New Testaments as the "Four Hundred Silent Years." These centuries are so designated not because God was not active in the affairs of men and nations, but because no known word came from God during that period of time. Luke recorded the breaking of that divine silence when the angel Gabriel appeared in the Temple one day to reveal some important truth to an old priest.

Our attention is directed by Luke to the city of Jerusalem and to an old priest, Zacharias, and his wife, Elizabeth. Elizabeth and Zacharias were both of the priestly tribe of Levi and both were "advanced in years" (1:7), that is, they were past the age of sixty. Also, both of them were said to be righteous, carefully walking according to the law of God. They were godly people. It is noteworthy to observe that in these first chapters of Luke God selected only those godly individuals through whom He would work out His purposes. God's standards have not changed. He commits His significant work to those who love Him, fear Him, and obey Him.

Zacharias was a priest of the order of Abijah (1:5). King David had established twenty-four divisions within the priesthood in order to make things more orderly and proper (1 Chron. 6:31-32). This meant, in the time of Zacharias, that a priest would come and serve for two weeks out of the year at the Jerusalem Temple. By the time of Zacharias, the priesthood had grown so large that the special ministry opportunity of serving at the altar of incense, inside the Holy Place of the Temple, occurred only once in a priest's lifetime.[1]

The gospel of Luke opens focusing on that special day in the life of righteous Zacharias when he was chosen to place incense on the altar (symbolic of the prayers of God's people). While he was inside the Temple, in the Holy Place, the early morning worshipers were offering their prayers to God. It was then that the angel Gabriel appeared to the old priest with the wonderful news that God was about to act in fulfillment of many Old Testament prophecies (1:11). After calming the natural fears of Zacharias, Gabriel told him that God was going to answer the prayers of the priest and his wife. They had for years prayed for a child (1:13). But this child was to be not an ordinary child. This child was to be the prophesied forerunner of the long-awaited Messiah (Isa. 40:3; Mal. 3:1).

Gabriel then told the amazed priest some truths about this child (1:15-17). This child, who would be named John ("the Lord is gracious") and would be a Nazirite from birth (see Num. 6:1-8 for the Nazirite vow). He would be controlled by the Holy Spirit even before his birth. He would be instrumental in pointing many Israelites to God and preparing a remnant of

1. Alfred Edersheim, *The Life and Times of Jesus the Messiah,* 2 vols. (New York: Longmans, Green, 1900), 1:133-35.

people for the appearing of the Messiah. Also, he would be very similar in character and fearlessness to the prophet Elijah. Overwhelmed by this message, Zacharias responded in unbelief (1:18). It was not every day that an angel appeared to him, yet the priest did not believe and asked for further evidence. Zacharias's wish was granted. Gabriel gave him a sign. He was struck dumb (1:20) and deaf (1:62). He would not be able to communicate in a normal manner until the birth of John.

The worshipers on the outside realized that something had happened inside the Temple. Not only was Zacharias long overdue in coming out again, but when he did come out he tried to talk to them, but remained speechless. This was the first of several incidents designed to cause the people of Israel to sense that God was beginning to act. Upon completing his priestly duties, Zacharias returned to his village near Jerusalem and no doubt wrote out in great detail all that had transpired, so that Elizabeth would understand that the divine silence of the centuries had been broken. Soon it became clear that Elizabeth miraculously was pregnant. She rejoiced that her "disgrace" (1:25) was taken away. It was commonly believed that to be childless was a mark of God's disfavor on a life that was displeasing to Him. No doubt Zacharias and Elizabeth had suffered many unkind remarks during their long lives. But now God was going to honor in a great way this righteous couple, illustrating once again that many of man's religious concepts are not accurate at all.

2. The announcement of the birth of Jesus (1:26-38). In the sixth month of Elizabeth's pregnancy (1:24, 26), Gabriel made his second appearance. The focus of attention now shifted to the little village of Nazareth and to a young girl by the name of Mary. Mary was engaged to a man named Joseph. Both of them were from the tribe of Judah and the line of King David. A young girl, like Mary, was usually betrothed between twelve and twelve and a half.[2] The betrothal ceremony began the

2. Joachim Jeremias, *Jerusalem in the Time of Jesus* (Philadelphia: Fortress, 1969), pp. 363-65.

transfer of the girl from the authority of her father to the authority of her husband. If the situation of Mary and Joseph was normal, Mary was probably in her early teens when Gabriel appeared to her with the news that she was to be the mother of the Messiah.

Mary's initial response was similar to that of the priest Zacharias. Gabriel found it necessary to calm her fears (1:30). Twice Gabriel stated that Mary found favor with God (1:28, 30). What is it that causes people to please God? According to Hebrews 11:6, it is faith. It can be stated then that Mary was a young girl who had learned to trust in God and in His revealed Word. Her trust in God is also revealed in her reaction to the message from God through the angel. When informed that she was to be the mother of the Messiah, she submitted herself to the will of God even though she had questions as to how it would be accomplished (1:38).

Mary stands in contrast to Zacharias. He questioned the fact of the birth, Mary did not. Zacharias had some precedent in the Old Testament for aged persons becoming parents; Mary had no precedent for a virgin birth. Zacharias asked for further evidence; Mary did not. She was a girl of great faith.

Gabriel told Mary that the conception of the child would be a miraculous thing. Normal sexual relations would not be involved, but rather the creator God would generate life within her womb (1:35). Her child would be not only her physical son (truly man), but He would be the Son of God (truly deity). Furthermore, Mary was given an unasked-for sign as evidence. Her sign was the pregnancy of Elizabeth (1:36). And Mary immediately accepted the will of God for her life.

Gabriel also informed Mary about the work of her son. He was to be called Jesus ("the Lord is salvation"), which pictured His great work of redeeming mankind. He would reign on the throne of David over the nation of Israel in a kingdom that would last forever. This declaration by Gabriel (1:32-33) reflects the many Old Testament promises that Messiah would reign upon the earth in a glorious kingdom. The great Davidic Covenant (2 Sam. 7) will be fulfilled someday when Christ comes a second time and rules upon the earth. The words of Gabriel will have their ultimate fulfillment at that time.

3. The journey of Mary to the home of Elizabeth (1:39-56). Shortly after the angel Gabriel appeared to Mary, she left Nazareth in Galilee and journeyed to some small town in the hill country of Judea (1:39). Gabriel's appearance profoundly affected her, and she sought confirmation of his words. Most likely Mary went to seek that confirming sign of Elizabeth's pregnancy, but it may well be that she wished the counsel of this godly older woman.

Mary not only received confirmation of Gabriel's sign, but also another clear evidence that God had spoken to her. This second sign was the prophecy of Elizabeth. Elizabeth, being a righteous woman, knew the Scriptures. She knew that if she was the mother of one who would announce the Messiah, then Messiah Himself would appear shortly. But she would not know when or where. When Mary arrived at her home, the Holy Spirit in an instant revealed to Elizabeth that her relative Mary was to have that exalted privilege of being the mother of Messiah. Before Mary could reveal one thing about her own experience, Elizabeth declared prophetically Mary's special and wonderful place in God's plans (1:41-45).

Mary had come to seek confirmation of a sign and received two evidences from God that His Word would be fulfilled about her. Her response was that of praise. First, Mary described how she felt about this situation that she had been placed in (1:46-48). She acknowledged her need of a savior. Second, she praised the Person of God for His wonderful deeds, great power and holiness, and the fact that He shows mercy to those (like Mary and Elizabeth) who fear Him (1:49-50). Her hymn of praise reached a climax (1:51-53) as she praised God for the way He entered the history of man and exalted those who evidenced humility and who served Him. Finally, Mary pointed out that all she stated was based on the fact that God is true to His promises, especially to His great covenant with Abraham.

Mary then stayed with Elizabeth for three months. During that time they probably talked a great deal about the marvelous truths of the Old Testament that they were a part of. Most likely Mary returned home after she witnessed the birth of John.

4. The birth of John the Baptist (1:57-80). The obvious graciousness of God was seen when Elizabeth gave birth to her first and only son, John. Her friends and relatives observed correctly that this was the good hand of God upon Zacharias and Elizabeth, and they rejoiced with them.

The eighth day after the birth of a male child was a significant day. It was the day on which the child was circumcised according to the Mosaic commandment (Lev. 12:2-4). It was also the day when, according to custom, the child was named. This custom of naming the child on the day of his circumcision was probably based on the life of Abraham. When God gave him his new name (from Abram to Abraham), God also commanded him to be circumcised as a sign of the covenant that had been made (Gen. 17:4-11).

The friends who had gathered on this significant day assumed that the baby would be called Zacharias. That was to be expected since this was certainly going to be the only child for this aged couple. However, the relatives were taken back when Elizabeth informed them that the baby would be named John. Undoubtedly Zacharias had written this information to Elizabeth many months before the birth of the child. Zacharias sat in his isolated world of deafness and dumbness and observed the proceedings. He knew, of course, what day it was. Since the friends and relatives could not ask him any questions verbally, they made signs and gestured to communicate the question "What is the name of the child?" He wrote that he was to be called John. The relatives were amazed that he would agree to that name, but they were even more amazed when, after nine months of silence, Zacharias began to speak. Zacharias had had many months of isolation to contemplate the words of Gabriel and the words of the Old Testament writers. Zacharias had initially responded in unbelief. But faith comes from hearing the Word of God. Zacharias now responded in faith, and that faith loosened his tongue.

He praised God and prophesied of things yet to come. He praised God for keeping His promises to Israel (1:68), for bringing salvation to His people (1:68-69), and for remembering His covenant commitments to Israel, those covenants made with Abraham and David (1:69, 73). Zacharias also looked into the future and spoke of what his son, John, would do (1:76-79). John would make many in Israel realize that their self-righteousness had alienated them from God and that they needed to turn back to God and receive the forgiveness of sins. Then these repentant ones would be prepared for the Messiah.

Luke concluded his account of the birth of John the Baptist with a summary verse about John's life before he came into the public eye. It is not said how long a time he spent in the desert regions or if he lived in isolation during this time. It is very doubtful that John had any intimate contact with the Qumran community, that group near the Dead Sea responsible for the "Dead Sea scrolls." This group's theology and practice differed radically from the known ministry of John the Baptist. But it is known from Luke that this was a time during which John was prepared more fully for the unique ministry given to him by God.

5. The birth of Jesus (2:1-52). After the birth of John, Mary journeyed back to Nazareth. It was probably at this time that she attempted to explain to Joseph about her own pregnancy (some four months along by now). Matthew's gospel records the struggle that Joseph had with that news and his decision to divorce Mary (Matt. 1:18-20). But after divine revelation, Joseph realized the truth of Mary's story and immediately took her to be his wife, thus affording her protection.

Luke then picks up the story at the time of the actual birth of Jesus. Luke informs us that God used a Roman decree to move Joseph and Mary from Nazareth to Bethlehem in order to fulfill the prophecy regarding the birthplace of the Messiah (Mic. 5:2). He states that this decree was given "in those days"

(2:1), which roughly refers to the time of the birth of John.

There is a technical problem related to the mentioning of Quirinius as the governor of Syria (2:2). The birth of Jesus took place about 5 B.C., yet Quirinius did not become governor until about A.D. 6, or about eleven years after the birth of Jesus. Yet Luke says that Quirinius was governor at the time of Jesus' birth. Some have attempted to solve this problem by stating that Quirinius was actually governor on two different occasions, the first one being around the birth of Christ and the second one being in A.D. 6.[3] Although some support can be brought forth for this view, there are many problems with it. A better solution has to do with the way in which the verse is actually translated. After dealing with a number of lines of evidence, Harold Hoehner states,

> The Greek means, "This census took place before Quirinius was governor of Syria." Luke is not distinguishing an earlier census from one during the governorship of Quirinius, but is merely stating that the census at the time of the nativity took place some time before Quirinius held office. This gives good sense to the passage at hand.[4]

There was a well-known decree in the time of Quirinius, and all Luke is doing is telling his readers that the decree related to the nativity occurred before Quirinius ever took office.

The Lord uses many things to accomplish His purposes. In this case He used the unwelcome decree of a hated government in order to fulfill His ancient prophecy that the Messiah would be born in Bethlehem of Judea. Mary and Joseph arrived in Bethlehem along with many others who came because of the decree of Caesar. A small town like Bethlehem was not prepared to accommodate so large a crowd at one time. The

3. Everett F. Harrison, *A Short Life of Christ* (Grand Rapids: Eerdmans, 1968), p. 37.
4. Harold W. Hoehner, *Chronological Aspects of the Life of Christ* (Grand Rapids: Zondervan, 1978), pp. 18-23.

result was that Joseph and Mary found no housing. And seemingly to complicate matters, the time arrived for the birth of the child. Evidently they took refuge in one of the limestone caves that dot the area, and it was in a place used to keep animals that the Son of God was born. Mary placed her newborn son in a manger (feeding trough), and it was here that some shepherds found the Messiah.

These shepherds had been out in the nearby fields keeping watch over their flocks when an angel with great glory appeared to them. The angel informed them that Messiah had been born in Bethlehem (2:9-11). The appearance of one angel had frightened these men, and the subsequent appearance of tens of thousands of angels chanting glory to God no doubt absolutely overwhelmed them. When the angels disappeared and when the shepherds recovered they went and found the baby, the Messiah. These humble shepherds became the first human announcers of the Messiah. And once again God saw fit to exalt the humble (1:52).

Luke noted that Jesus was the "firstborn" son of Mary (2:7). His selection of this word tells us that Mary did have other children and was not perpetually a virgin. It must be remembered that Luke wrote fifty years after the event and certainly knew if Mary and Joseph had other children.

The events during the first weeks after the birth of Jesus were very special to Mary, and she thought a great deal about them (2:19), an indication that Luke's information for this portion came from Mary herself. Following the encouragement of the shepherd's visit, God gave further confirmations in the days that followed.

On the eighth day the rite of circumcision was performed, which gave testimony to their belief in the Abrahamic covenant. And according to custom, the child was officially named on that day. But Mary, according to the law (Lev. 12:4-8), was ceremonially unclean for thirty-three days after the circumcision of Jesus. When that period of time was over certain purification rites were required (2:22-24). It was also necessary to redeem the firstborn child, and that was also done (Ex. 13:2;

Num. 3:13). The using of birds as sacrificial animals was legal but did indicate the poverty of Mary and Joseph.

In spite of the low spiritual condition in the nation of Israel at that time, there were still some godly people looking for God to deliver His people. Luke introduces his readers to two such individuals, Anna and Simeon. Simeon (2:25) was told by God that he would not die until he had the opportunity to see Messiah, the One who would deliver Israel. The Lord led him into the Temple on that day when Joseph and Mary were fulfilling the requirements of the law. Simeon took the baby in his arms and thanked God. He also amazed Joseph and Mary with his declaration that the salvation brought by this One would extend to the Gentiles (2:32). They evidently had not contemplated that before.

The second pious individual mentioned by Luke was an old woman by the name of Anna. This prophetess saw Messiah and spent her days in the Temple telling all that He had come (2:38).

At this point, Luke seems to indicate that after the Temple presentation, the family returned to Nazareth (2:39-40). But Luke is simply summarizing matters as he does periodically in his gospel (for example, 1:80). Luke leaves out their short stay in Bethlehem, the visit of the wise men, and the flight to Egypt.

The only information about the childhood years of Jesus is to be found in this next section of Luke's gospel (2:40-52). Luke gives to us a glimpse of the humanity of Jesus as he relates an event that took place when Jesus was twelve years of age.

It was probably the custom of Joseph and Mary, as devout Jews, to go to Jerusalem every year for the Passover feast. When Jesus was twelve they once again made the journey. It was customary for large groups of pilgrims to travel together for safety. The women would go on ahead with the younger children, and the men would follow in another group. As Joseph and Mary returned from the feast in Jerusalem, Joseph probably assumed that Jesus was with Mary and the children, and Mary assumed that Jesus, now twelve and a man, was with

Joseph. He was with neither one. With the natural anxiety of parents they anxiously returned to Jerusalem seeking Jesus. After three days (2:46) they found Him in the Temple. Those in the Temple were amazed by His keen insight and understanding of God's truth—a demonstration of Jesus' unfallen mind at work. Jesus' parents rebuked Him for His apparent unconcern for them. But He responded by reminding them of the priorities that He had in His life. It is difficult to know how much Jesus understood about Himself and His future ministry at this time. Obediently He returned with Mary and Joseph.

Luke's summary statement (2:52) is quite significant. In it the natural and normal development of Jesus the man is revealed. Jesus experienced normal growth in all areas of His life. He grew in wisdom (mental growth), stature (physical growth), in favor with God (spiritual growth), and in favor with man (social growth). When Jesus was five years old, He was a perfect five-year-old. At five He was not a spiritual or mental twenty-five-year-old. When Jesus was fourteen, He was a perfect fourteen-year-old, but not a thirty-year-old. He was fully and completely a human being.

Evidently no one thought of Him as unusual or anything more than a common man. The people of His day certainly did not point to Him and exclaim, "There is God!" Later in the ministry of Jesus, Peter declared that Jesus was indeed the Son of God (Matt. 16:16). Jesus confirmed that declaration to be true but explained that that perception came about by means of divine illumination. Luke's gospel emphasizes the true and complete humanity of Jesus. It must be remembered, however, that Jesus Christ was (and is) the God-man. He was (and is) perfect humanity and full and complete deity, united in one Person forever. As He walked this earth, the God-man possessed all the attributes of God. He simply chose not to use them and also to veil His glory. The apostle Paul explains that it was the *external manifestation* of His deity that He laid aside when He became a man (Phil. 2:5-8) and not His attributes of deity. In Luke's gospel, Jesus is seen as a perfect human being. That perfect humanity gives some insights into what mankind lost when he plunged into sin soon after his creation (Gen. 3:1-7; Rom. 5:12-21).

After the brief account of Jesus as a twelve-year-old, there exist eighteen years of silence in the record. Not until Jesus was about thirty years old does the narrative continue. Although there is no history from this time period, certain suggestions can be made. During these years Jesus was trained as a carpenter. He undoubtedly worked alongside Joseph for many years. Later on, after His ministry had begun, Jesus was called *the* carpenter (not the carpenter's son), which strongly suggests that Joseph had died sometime during those eighteen years (Mark 6:3). If so, then Jesus probably became responsible for the family, as the eldest son. This is also supported by the fact that Joseph's name is never mentioned in the gospel narratives dealing with the ministry of Jesus.

Also, it can be stated that no miracles were performed by Jesus during those eighteen years. He did not work His first miracle until He was actually ministering (John 2). Everything points to those eighteen years as normal and usual, devoid of the extraordinary.

So Luke began his gospel by recording the announcements of the two special births and then the births themselves. He will now proceed to discuss the period of the preparation for the ministry of Jesus, the Son of Man.

B. HIS PRESENTATION TO ISRAEL (3:1—4:13)

1. The forerunner of Jesus (3:1-20). In these twenty verses, Luke summarizes the entire ministry of John the Baptist from his emergence out of the wilderness to his imprisonment by Herod. Other gospels fill in the details of John's ministry.

Luke begins this section by giving six chronological notations (3:1-2) in order to date the beginning of John's ministry. The only precise date out of the six is the one placing the commencement of John's ministry in the fifteenth year of Tiberias Caesar, which would most likely be the year A.D. 29.[5]

5. Ibid., p. 37.

The movement of John the Baptist was a separatist movement; that is, it was outside of the established religion of Judaism, and it did not have the official approval of the religious leaders. The religious leaders quickly learned about John and went to investigate him (John 1:19-28). They wondered if he was the Messiah. He declared that he was not, but that he was simply "the voice of one crying in the wilderness" (Isa. 40:3). As the weeks went by, more and more people were attracted to John's message of repentance and his ministry of water baptism. In a relatively few months John had attained a great influence over the nation, an influence that worried both secular and religious leaders. Josephus, a Jewish historian of that time, recorded Herod's uneasiness about John the Baptist.

> Now, when (many) others came to crowd about him, for they were greatly moved (or pleased) by hearing his words, Herod, who feared lest the great influence John had over the people might put it into his power and inclination to raise a rebellion, (for they seemed ready to do anything he should advise), thought it best, by putting him to death, to prevent any mischief he might cause, and not bring himself into difficulties, by sparing a man who might make him repent of it when it should be too late.[6]

The religious leaders resisted John and became a target for some of his pointed statements (Matt. 3:7).

John's message was designed to prepare the nation of Israel for the prophesied Messiah. The nation was to repent of (change its attitude and turn away from) its sins and identify itself with the Messiah, who was coming to establish His kingdom. That kingdom, John declared, was "at hand" (Matt. 3:2). What kingdom? The kingdom that fulfilled the great Davidic and Abrahamic covenants (2 Sam. 7; Gen. 12, 15, 17).

6. Flavius Josephus, *Josephus,* trans. William Whiston (Grand Rapids: Kregel, 1971), p. 382.

It was to be a literal, earthly kingdom that Messiah would rule over (note again Gabriel's statement in Luke 1:32-33). Although there would be spiritual aspects to this kingdom, it was not a "spiritual kingdom" (the rule of God in the hearts of His people). A "spiritual kingdom" had always existed. John was announcing the nearness of another aspect of the kingdom: the earthly kingdom of Messiah. The actual arrival of this earthly kingdom depended upon a positive response by the people of Israel. Only Israel's unrepentance could stop it from coming at that time (which is what happened). John the Baptist's message was designed to bring about that needed repentance.

John's ministry included water baptism as an external sign of inward repentance. John did not originate the methodology of water baptism, as it was used by other groups at that time, such as the Pharisees and the Essenes. The word *bapto* means "to dip" or "to dye" (used in the trade of a fuller, or dyer of cloth). The word was used to refer to putting cloth into a pot of dye. The cloth then became the color of the dye—it changed its identity. When one is baptized, he is identified with a particular group, movement, or person. John used baptism as a means of identifying people with the coming Messiah.

His baptism was one of repentance. John's baptism could not forgive and remove sins, since the Scriptures clearly teach that the removal of sin is based on blood, not water. The removal of sin begins with repentance, and baptism is the outward declaration that the person has a new spiritual identity. John demanded that those who wished to be baptized give some evidence that they had indeed repented of their sins (3:10-14). He warned the nation of Israel not to depend on its religion, ancestry, or even its covenant relation with God through Abraham (3:8). If the nation did not repent, then the nation would face the judgment of God (3:9).

Evidently John had to continually declare that he was not the Messiah, but simply His forerunner (3:15). So much greater was the coming Messiah that John was unworthy to perform the tasks of a servant (3:16). John taught the people that

Messiah would baptize them in the Holy Spirit and with fire. The baptizing in the Holy Spirit looked forward to the life that would be received through the Spirit's regeneration of man. The fire is symbolic of God's judgment and is so used in the Old Testament (for example, Ezek. 20:47; Joel 2:30). All the people would be "baptized" by Messiah, either with life or with judgment. Later on, Jesus would say much the same thing in John 5:21-24. John's use of fire as a reference to judgment is seen in his illustration of the threshing floor (3:17).

Luke concludes his summary of John the Baptist's ministry by telling of John's imprisonment. Luke will again speak about John later on in his gospel (7:18-35).

2. The baptism of Jesus (3:21-22). Luke's account of the baptism of Jesus is an abbreviated one. Luke simply informs us that Jesus, along with many others, went and was baptized by John. He does not inform us, as Matthew does, that John initially strongly objected to the idea of Jesus being baptized by him. John was persuaded, however, when he understood that his ministry was really an extension of the Old Testament requirements. Just as it was necessary for Jesus to be circumcised and attend the prescribed feasts, so it was necessary for Him to be baptized (Matt. 3:15). John understood that Jesus did not have anything to repent of but did not realize that Jesus needed to be baptized to fulfill all of the law's requirements.

Luke records that the Holy Spirit came upon Jesus at the moment of His baptism. This visible manifestation was given in order that men might see and understand that Jesus was anointed by the Spirit. His anointing was His induction into the office of king. Just as kings in the Old Testament were anointed with oil (symbolizing the Holy Spirit) at the time of their inauguration, so Jesus was anointed by the Spirit Himself as He was inaugurated as Israel's king, fulfilling the Davidic covenant. The dove fulfilled Isaiah 42:1. Christ spoke of this (Luke 4:18) when He taught from Isaiah 61:1 in the synagogue at Nazareth. The voice from heaven was a kind of coronation formula for the king (Ps. 2:7-8).

3. The genealogy of Jesus (3:23-38). There has been some difficulty regarding this genealogy found in Luke. Some have seen it as that of Joseph[7] and others as that of Mary.[8] Although either view is acceptable, it is probably better to hold that the genealogy recorded in Luke is that of Mary. Luke had already stated that Jesus was the son of Mary only. It is rather useless and perhaps even misleading to now give Joseph's genealogy (Matthew gives the genealogy of Joseph). It is more likely that Luke is giving the *real* (and not the legal) genealogy of Jesus, since he is emphasizing Jesus' humanity. The genealogical table of Joseph simply does not fit in with Luke's purpose.[9]

In the genealogical section, Luke once again gives a helpful time notation (3:23). He states that Jesus was "about thirty years of age" when He began to enter the public eye. Since Jesus was only six months younger than John the Baptist and since John began his ministry in A.D. 29, it is therefore quite likely that Jesus began His ministry in late A.D. 29.[10] If this was the case, it means that Jesus was around thirty-two or thirty-three when he began His ministry. (With a ministry of a little over three years, He would have been about thirty-six when He was crucified.) Traditionally it has been held that Jesus was exactly thirty when He began His ministry. But Luke does use the term *about* which allows for some flexibility.[11]

4. The testing of Jesus (4:1-13). After He was baptized by John in the Jordan River, Jesus was led by the Spirit into the Judean wilderness area (Mark says that it was "immediately" after His baptism; Mark 1:12). The traditionally thought place for the temptation of Jesus is a barren and desolate area near the Dead Sea. For a period of forty days Satan attempted to get

7. Alfred Plummer, *A Critical and Exegetical Commentary on the Gospel According to St. Luke,* 3d ed. (Edinburgh: T. and T. Clark, 1900), p. 103.
8. A. T. Robertson, *A Harmony of the Gospels for Students of the Life of Christ* (New York: Harper and Bros., 1922), p. 259.
9. Norval Geldenhuys, *Commentary on the Gospel of Luke* (Grand Rapids: Eerdmans, 1966), p. 152.
10. Hoehner, p. 38.
11. Ibid., p. 38.

Jesus to sin. The temptations were far more extensive than the three recorded by Luke and the other synoptic gospels. Luke is clear that the temptation experience went on throughout the entire forty day period (4:2). The three recorded temptations took place *after* the forty days of temptation. In fact, Luke makes clear that Satan did not stop testing the Lord Jesus in the wilderness but continued on throughout His life (4:13, "until an opportune time"). Hebrews 2:18 and 4:15 lend support to the idea that Jesus was the target of satanic attack at all times and in every possible way.

But information about this specific time of temptation was given in order to present unmistakable evidence that Jesus was morally and spiritually qualified to be the Messiah and the redeemer of mankind. Jesus met Satan in the most unfavorable circumstances and came out victorious (in contrast with Adam, who sinned in the most favorable of circumstances).

Jesus did not sin. But the question is often raised, Could He have sinned? The answer is a definite no. It is true that Jesus' unfallen human nature could have fallen under Satan's many temptations (Adam had an unfallen nature, and he succumbed to the temptation of Satan). But Jesus did not possess just an unfallen human nature; He also possessed the very nature of God. The *Person* of Jesus Christ could not have sinned. The human nature made it possible for Jesus to be *tempted,* but the divine nature made it impossible for Him to sin (He was impeccable). He could have "felt" the pull of temptations upon His humanity, but as the God-man, holy and righteous, He could not have yielded. The purpose of the temptation was not to see if Jesus would or would not sin. It was to demonstrate openly to men and angels the righteous character of the Son of Man.

The synoptic gospels all record the three temptations of the Lord Jesus that took place after the forty-day period. Jesus Himself must have been the source of this information, since it is highly unlikely that Satan would want to disclose this wonderful account of Christ's victory.

In the first temptation, Satan used Jesus' natural hunger (after going forty days without eating) to raise doubt as to His divine Sonship (4:3). Satan suggested that He turn stones into bread in order to prove the truth of God's declaration "Thou art My beloved Son" (3:22). This temptation was directed at a primary prerequisite for the Messiah, that of complete faith in and total dependence upon God. Jesus refused to act independently of God. Jesus responded to Satan with the Word of God, pointing out that the most important thing in life is to be rightly related to God; and bread, though important, is secondary. (Matthew 4:11 records that God did indeed provide for Jesus).

In the second recorded temptation, Satan, through some means, showed Jesus the kingdoms of the world (4:5). He offered to give those kingdoms to Jesus if He would worship Satan. (They were Satan's to give; see John 12:31; 14:30; 16:11.) Without having to fight, struggle, or die, Jesus could reign. Again quoting the Scriptures, Jesus rejected Satan's temptation, reminding him to keep his place as a created being.

In the third temptation, Satan invited Jesus to jump off of the pinnacle (a tower that was a part of the wall surrounding the Temple area) of the Jerusalem Temple. Satan, by now noting that Jesus had a great loyalty to the Scriptures, quoted Scripture himself. It was Satan's suggestion that Jesus could experience a shortcut to success if He threw Himself from the pinnacle and then was rescued by God's angels. Certainly those observing would acclaim Him as Messiah. Jesus, once again using God's Word, responded by pointing out that testing God is not trusting God. By this time Satan had tried "every possible kind of temptation" and left the battlefield defeated.

Temptation is the stirring up of natural desires to go beyond the boundaries set up by God in His Word. In order for believers in Christ to resist temptation we must have a working knowledge of the Word of God. Only in the Scriptures are we able to see clearly God's perspective on life. Only with this perspective can we adequately deal with the pressures, testings, and problems that we face. It is good to remember two basic

facts about temptation when it comes our way: (1) We do have a High Priest, Jesus, who has personally experienced temptation and can give us power to win our spiritual battle (Heb. 4:14-16), and (2) God does censor all temptations to insure that nothing comes into our lives that will destroy us (1 Cor. 10:13). Satan cannot do anything he desires with us. We are followers of the Victor.

After discussing the important facts about the preparation for the ministry of Jesus, Luke turns his attention to the actual ministry of Jesus the Son of Man.

2

THE MINISTRY OF JESUS THE SON OF MAN

(LUKE 4:14—9:50)

A. HIS MINISTRY BEGINS (4:14-30)

As Luke begins his record of the ministry of the Son of Man, he gives two general verses about that ministry. Luke mentions the two major elements of Jesus' ministry, His teaching and His miracle working ("the power of the Spirit"). Why was He fairly well known and "praised by all" (4:15)? Matthew records the fact that at this time He was performing many miracles of healing and was casting out many demons (Matt. 4:23-25). But it is important to recognize that Luke's summary verses (4:14-15) are actually summarizing a full year of the Lord's ministry. Matthew, Mark, and Luke do not include the first year of Christ's ministry (see fig. I.2). Only John records information about the early ministry of Christ. Therefore, between Luke 4:13 and 4:14 there exists about one year of ministry. It is difficult to say why Luke chose to begin at this point. It is true that the Lord Jesus' ministry in Galilee was the most significant time in terms of His miracle working, His teaching, and the growing opposition to Him from the religious establishment.

The first specific account given by Luke takes place in Jesus' hometown of Nazareth. In the record of the Lord's return to His hometown we note the beginning of the fulfillment of Simeon's prophecy (2:34-35) that not all would open their arms to Mary's son. There would be opposition to Him. Jesus came on the Sabbath to the synagogue. (See the "Additional Note" on

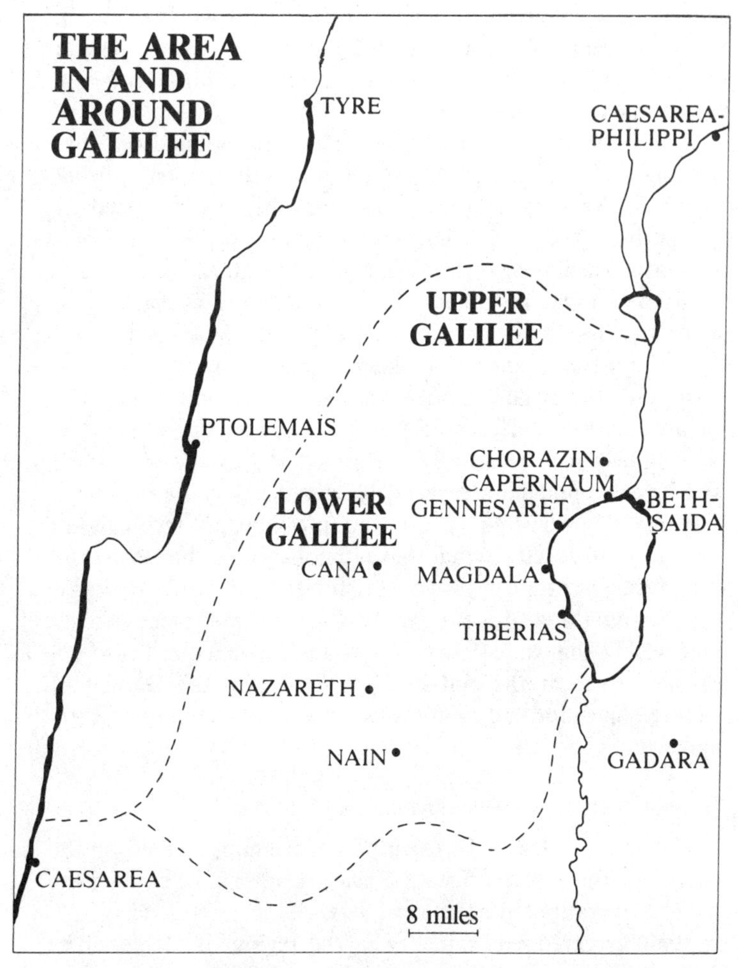

Fig. 2.1

the *synagogue* at the end of this chapter.) After reading from Isaiah 61, Jesus proclaimed that He was the fulfiller of this Scripture. Luke obviously gives a simple summary statement (4:21). Disbelief was the general response of the hearers as they reflected on the fact that Jesus had lived and worked among them for years without any hint that He was the Messiah (4:22). They had heard stories of impressive miracles being worked at Capernaum.

Jesus confronted their unbelief. First, He pointed out that blessing was conditioned on faith and that their open unbelief was the direct cause of miracles not being performed at Nazareth (4:23-24). Second, Jesus pointed to the Old Testament as a warning to them to change their attitude of unbelief. He used two Old Testament illustrations that took place in the general vicinity of Galilee. Elijah and the widow of Sidon and Elisha and the cleansing of Naaman both showed that when Israel failed to believe God, then God turned and blessed the Gentiles. Jesus in effect told the synagogue attenders that they were unbelievers because they rejected His messianic claims. The listeners understood perfectly what Jesus said and reacted violently. They desired to hurt Him (probably not trying to kill Him yet). Luke tells us that they did not succeed, however, and that Jesus went on His way (4:30). It is difficult to know whether anything of a supernatural nature took place here. It may well be that such "escapes" took place on a number of occasions, since at the end of His ministry in the Garden of Gethsemane, Judas Iscariot was concerned that the soldiers make sure they kept Him securely (Mark 14:44).

B. HIS AUTHORITY DEMONSTRATED (4:31—6:11)

The scene shifts to the town of Capernaum, located on the northern shore of the Sea of Galilee. Capernaum became the base of operations for the Lord Jesus.

Jesus centered His ministry in the region of Galilee. The Jews of Galilee in some respects were quite different from the Jews of Judea. And noting a few of these differences helps to explain some of the divergent attitudes toward Jesus as well as the variation of ministry that Jesus had in those two regions.

The Galileans were viewed as "country cousins" by those from Jerusalem and Judea. Jerusalem was the center of Jewish learning, Jewish religious life, and political power. Undisguised contempt for the Galileans is reflected in the saying "If anyone wishes to be rich let him go north; if he wants to be wise, let him come south."[1]

> Indeed, what we know of the Galileans would quite prepare us for expecting that the gospel should have received at least a ready hearing among many of them. . . . they seem to have been a warm-hearted, impulsive, generous race—intensely national in the best sense, active, not given to idle speculations. . . . They show more earnest practical piety and strictness of life, and less adherence to those Pharisaical distinctions which so often made void the law.[2]

The Galileans strictly kept the law but were basically indifferent to the traditionalism of the Judeans. This traditionalism, of course, was a key point of conflict between Jesus and the religious leaders from Judea. His violation of their rules and regulations was one of the basic reasons for their rejection of Him.

It is also true that the Galileans were more open to the miracles that He performed.

> Furthermore, the Galileans were more prone to accept miracles and faith healing than were the Jews of Judaea. Even among the Rabbis this was known.[3]

And the vast majority of the recorded miracles of Christ took place in the region of Galilee.

By noting these few, brief generalities about the Galilean and Judean Jews, it is clearer why the greatest outpouring of Jesus' miracles took place in Galilee and why Jesus' denunciation of

1. Alfred Edersheim, *Sketches of Jewish Social Life in the Days of Christ* (Grand Rapids: Eerdmans, 1967), p. 30.
2. Ibid., p. 39.
3. Harold Hoehner, *Herod Antipas* (Grand Rapids: Zondervan, 1980), p. 60.

traditionalism was accepted there. It is also understandable why the Jewish establishment of Judea was immediately suspicious of this Jesus from Nazareth in Galilee and that they tended to reject both His message and His miracles.

As Luke opens his record of the great Galilean ministry of Jesus Christ, he details a number of different areas where the Lord's authority was demonstrated.

1. His authority over demons (4:31-37). First John 3:8 states that the Lord Jesus came to destroy the works of the devil. One thing Satan does in order to expand his own kingdom and resist the kingdom of God is to control human beings. Demons (fallen angels) take control of the faculties of a man. This control manifests itself in a variety of ways. But no matter what the manifestation, the demon is more powerful than the man and always resists expulsion from him. A concise summary of these beings is given in the following quote.

> Demons are persons with intellect, sensibility, and will, just as are angels. They are spirit beings who are morally perverted in their personality, in their doctrine, and in their conduct. Often they are called unclean spirits or evil spirits. They are normally invisible but sometimes may appear in hideous forms. They possess powers of supernatural intelligence, strength, and presence. The totality of their personalities and powers is directed against God and in accord with Satan's leadership.[4]

In His ministry the Lord Jesus dealt with these wicked spirits on numerous occasions. In the synagogue at Capernaum, Jesus was teaching when a demon-controlled man yelled out, declaring that he knew that Jesus was the Holy One of God (4:34). The cry was one of surprise and terror as the demon realized that Christ could cast him out of the man and into a place of permanent confinement (Luke 8:31). The demon also evi-

4. C. Fred Dickason, *Angels Elect and Evil* (Chicago: Moody, 1975), pp. 167-68.

denced knowledge of Jesus' power and probably his own future in the lake of fire (Rev. 20:10), that place of eternal punishing prepared for Satan and the demons. The demon exhibited both emotion and intellect in this encounter.

Jesus' great authority was demonstrated in that He spoke briefly, but powerfully, to this evil being and said, "Be quiet [muzzled]" (4:35). The demon departed the man after throwing him to the ground. All the people who watched this spiritual battle were absolutely amazed at the authority demonstrated by Jesus. News of this event and others circulated throughout the area.

2. His authority over sickness and disease (4:38-44). Immediately after delivering the synagogue attender from the power of the demon, Jesus entered the house of Peter. It is thought by many that Peter's house was the base of operations for Jesus' ministry in Galilee. Peter's mother-in-law was seriously ill with a high fever. (It is obvious that Peter was married, since he had a mother-in-law and his wife accompanied him on his preaching tours years later; (1 Cor. 9:5.) The Lord Jesus spoke a word, and the fever was gone, and she was fully restored to health and strength. This is one characteristic of genuine, divine healing; it is complete and total. Also, it is instantaneous.*

Luke continues his narrative by telling, in summary fashion, something of the extent of Jesus' healing and delivering ministry (4:40-41). Jesus healed people of diseases that were from natural causes, and He cast out demons (with many diverse outward manifestations), which had supernatural powers. In both cases His great power was evidenced and pointed to Him as being the Messiah. It is important to note

*The only exception to instantaneous healing in the New Testament is found in Mark 8:23-26, where Jesus deliberately healed a blind man in two stages, with one stage following the other immediately. Since Christ's power was sufficient to heal immediately, Jesus was evidently using such an approach as a teaching device for the blind man or the disciples. Spiritually we need to be touched by Jesus in order to see more clearly spiritual truth.

that the primary purpose of Jesus' miracles was not to heal and deliver from evil spirits but rather to give clear evidence that He was sent from God and that His message was true. The miracles were designed to authenticate Him and His message. The Old Covenant came through Moses and was verified by great supernatural signs and miracles. Since God authenticated His revelation to Moses and Israel by means of miracles, it was necessary to give signs to verify the new revelation that came through Jesus Christ and the apostles. God-fearing Jews would look for such evidence (1 Cor. 1:22). The New Covenant came, and God once again allowed supernatural manifestations in order to give all the external evidence that was needed to authenticate the revelation.

It is also important to observe the kinds of miracles that Jesus worked. He could have done such supernatural feats as raising the Temple a hundred feet in the air or causing the Jordan River to flow up to the Sea of Galilee instead of down from it. The kind of miracles He worked pointed to the kingdom that He would establish. Satan would be defeated, and the effects of sin would be dealt with. Sickness and deformity would be absent from Messiah's kingdom according to passages like Isaiah 35. The kind of miracle Jesus performed and the great number of miracles He performed gave overwhelming evidence of His messiahship. And this is why the nation of Israel stood severely condemned later on when they rejected Him and denied that these miracles were from God.

As this section is concluded (4:43-44), the Lord Jesus was besieged by the crowds asking Him not to leave but to stay with them. Jesus informed them that He had to go and preach in other cities as well. These verses make clear that Jesus' primary ministry was to preach the truth of God and not to work miracles. It was the truth of God that changed lives. Miracles and healings could help validate the truth, but they could not produce faith. Faith comes by hearing and responding to the Word of God. Jesus' emphasis in His ministry should be ours as well.

3. His authority over nature (5:1-11). Luke does not give an exact time for this event, but it was probably early in the great Galilean ministry. Jesus wanted all of the large crowd that had gathered to be able to hear what He had to say. He requested Peter to push his boat off the beach and just a little way into the water (5:1-3). In this way Jesus could be heard by everyone as He taught. After completing His speaking Jesus intended to reward Peter for the "rental" of his boat, and to instruct him. Jesus told Peter to go out onto the lake and cast his net. Peter balked at the suggestion since he had finished with his fishing for the day. But he obeyed, and an unbelieveable catch was made (5:6-7). Peter and his companions were awestruck by this demonstration of the Lord's authority. Peter recognized the hand of God in Christ's miracle, and that caused him to recognize his own sinfulness.

A proper view of God in the life of a person always causes that one to be sensitive to his own sinfulness. In fact, a proper view of God is one of the greatest deterrents to sin in a person's life (Prov. 16:6). Jesus calmed the fears of Peter and the others and then issued a call to come and follow Him. The fishermen responded to the Lord's invitation, left everything, and followed Him (5:11).

This is not the first time these fishermen were called to follow Christ. The first invitation is recorded in John 1:35-51. It was given while several of them were followers of John the Baptist. A second invitation is recorded in Matthew 4:18, and then this third call in Luke 5:11. The Matthew 4 account and the Luke 5 account have enough differences to indicate that two distinct events are being viewed. For example, in Matthew, James and John are in the boats; in Luke the boats are at shore. In Matthew they are casting and mending their nets; in Luke the nets have been washed. In Matthew, Jesus is alone, and there is no mention of a great catch of fish. Luke, on the other hand, states that a multitude was with Jesus and that the miraculous catch of fish took place.

Evidently the followers (disciples) of Jesus initially followed

Him temporarily on short tours and then returned to their businesses. About halfway through His ministry, Jesus selected twelve, whom He called "apostles," and those then followed Him on a permanent basis.

4. His authority over leprosy (5:12-26). Lepers were outcasts of society. The rabbis taught that one must not get any closer than six feet to a leper and, if the wind was blowing from his direction, one should stay at least one hundred feet away. One rabbi would not even eat an egg that had been purchased in a street where there was a leper. Another prided himself on the fact that he always threw stones at lepers.[5] In view of statements like these, the actions of the Lord Jesus in speaking to and touching a leper were extraordinary.

The leper in this account approached Jesus (5:12). He had, no doubt, heard of the miracles that Jesus was doing and was convinced that Jesus could heal him too. He came and expressed his belief. Jesus willingly responded to this man, healed him, and then instructed him to fulfill the Mosaic law by going and being officially declared clean by the priest (Lev. 14:1-11). The man had to make proper sacrifice as well. By His sending the man to the priest, the priest would discover how he had been cleansed. This should have alerted the priests to the arrival of the Messiah.

Even with the constant demands of people and the pressing need to preach the gospel to other cities and towns, the Lord Jesus habitually took time to be alone and to pray (5:16). His ministry was characterized by prayer, and His disciples were impressed by the reality and quality of His prayer life (Luke 11:1). Prayer is an acknowledgement of dependence on God for life and ministry. Prayerlessness is the believer's declaration of independence from God.

As usual the Lord had a large crowd around Him as He taught (5:17). On this occasion He also had some representa-

5. Alfred Edersheim, *The Life and Times of Jesus the Messiah,* 2 vols. (New York: Longmans, Green, 1900), 1:495.

tives of organized religion present. The scribes (teachers of the law) and the Pharisees were often present when the Lord taught in order to discover what He taught and if unorthodox things were being proclaimed. (See "Additional Note" on the *scribes* and on the *Pharisees* at the end of this chapter.)

As with the leper, we have introduced here some individuals who were absolutely convinced that Jesus could heal—even heal one who was paralyzed. The crowd was great and evidently would not move aside for these men and the stretcher they carried (5:18). They climbed onto the roof, probably using an outside stairway, removed the tiles of the roof, and lowered the invalid down to a spot in front of Jesus. Jesus observed the faith of all these men, including the paralytic. Evidently the Lord Jesus immediately realized that the man's physical condition was closely connected with sin of which he was guilty. Jesus declared that his sins were forgiven (5:20). This points clearly to the fact that the man also had expressed faith in the Lord Jesus, or else Jesus would not and could not have forgiven his sin. Sin must be dealt with by the sinner himself.

This story also illustrates the fact that some sickness is a direct result of sin in a person's life (1 Cor. 11:30). In one sense all sickness is the result of sin. If sin had not become a part of the human experience, then sickness and disease would not be present either. But some sickness is brought upon an individual because of specific sin in his life. It should be noted that Christ did come to take away sin and its by-products. Someday, at the resurrection, the grip of disease will be broken and the bodies of believers will be fully and completely redeemed (Rom. 8:20-23). But until then, disease and death will be part of the human experience.

Jesus dealt with the root issue in the life of the paralytic. However, the Pharisees were disturbed by Jesus' statement (5:21). They were correct when they reasoned that only God can forgive sins. But they were in error when they thought Jesus was guilty of blasphemy. Jesus perceived that they questioned His statement, so He asked a question of His own (5:23). On the surface it is much easier to say, "Your sins are forgiven," than it is to say, "Rise up and walk." The latter is immediately verifiable. But no one can tell if one's sins have been forgiven. So it is easier *to say* that one's "sins have been forgiven." Then to verify His ability to forgive sins, He brought healing to the paralytic, and all who observed were amazed and glorified God.

5. *His authority over men (5:27-29).* Tax collectors were highly unpopular with the Jews. They were employed by Rome and were generally regarded as thieves. The tax collectors (publicans) could assign an inflated value to the goods being taxed and thus raise the taxes of an individual. This was commonly done, and most tax collectors became wealthy from pocketing the extra revenue.

Levi (also called Matthew) had his tax collection booth on the busiest road in Palestine, the only "truly international road of all those which passed through Palestine."[6] This site, near Capernaum, must have given Matthew exposure to the Lord Jesus on a number of previous occasions. Matthew had undoubtedly heard Jesus and been drawn to Him. Jesus knew that he was ripe for discipleship. Jesus called him to join with Him, and Matthew left everything and followed Jesus.

> Matthew must have been the richest of the apostles. We should not miss the quiet heroism involved in this. If following Jesus had not worked out for the fishermen, they could have returned to their trade without difficulty. But when Levi walked out of his job he was through. They would surely never take back a man who had simply abandoned his tax office. His following of Jesus was a final commitment.[7]

Matthew hosted a great dinner with Jesus as the honored guest. To this dinner he invited his friends, who were generally

6. Edersheim, *Sketches,* p. 42.
7. Leon Morris, *The Gospel According to St. Luke* (Grand Rapids: Eerdmans, 1982), p. 119.

viewed as the dregs of society. Matthew wanted his Lord to be their Lord.

6. His authority over men's traditions (5:30-39). Matthew's dinner could be called a success except for the Pharisees who seemed now to be present on most every occasion. They criticized the Lord Jesus for His willing association with such disreputable people as the tax collectors and their kind. Jesus, informed by His disciples of this criticism, responded by pointing out that sick people are the ones who need a doctor (5:31). These at the dinner were terribly ill spiritually and needed Him, the Great Physician. Jesus was not saying that the Pharisees were righteous, spiritually healthy, and in no need of Him (5:32). The Pharisees were just as sick as the tax collectors (and maybe more so), but they refused to acknowledge their spiritual needs. Years later, a regenerated Pharisee (the apostle Paul) would declare that the nation of Israel sought to become righteous through its own efforts and as a result missed obtaining God's righteousness provided through Jesus Christ (Rom. 10:3-4). The first step in obtaining victory over sin is the candid acknowledgement of sin's presence and power in the life.

The Pharisees were not through with the critical observations of Christ and His disciples. Something else bothered them. They raised the issue of fasting, noting that John's disciples fasted frequently as did the Pharisees' disciples, but Jesus' followers did not fast. Many of the Pharisees fasted two days out of the week as a part of their strict religious life (Luke 18:12). Jesus addressed this issue by observing that fasting is an external sign of sorrow and mourning, and as long as He was present with His disciples sorrow was not an appropriate attitude.

There was only one day in the Old Testament on which the entire nation of Israel was commanded to fast (to deny oneself temporarily of certain necessities of life, usually food). That special day was the Day of Atonement (Lev. 16:29-31; 23:27-29, where the phrase "to humble [afflict] one's soul" is the expression used to give the full meaning to fasting). Fasting became a common feature in Israeli religious life as a means of demonstrating sorrow and mourning. However, because men were sacrificing personal comfort when they fasted, the practice easily and quickly fostered spiritual pride, which was denounced by God (Zech. 7:3-7; Matt. 6:16). It is interesting that fasting is absent from the New Testament epistles, which guide the behavior of the believer today.

Jesus concluded this encounter with the Pharisees by giving two illustrations designed to communicate a single truth (5:36-39). He said that new wine is not put into old wineskins, and a new piece of cloth is not used to patch an old garment. Christ was telling the Pharisees that He came to introduce something new. It would be better than the old, and it simply could not become part of the old. To try to force His teachings into the old wineskins of Judaism (such as by imposition of fasting) would not be possible. Jesus then predicted that their response would be that the old is better (5:39).

7. His authority over the Sabbath (6:1-11). The Pharisees and scribes contended with the Lord Jesus over a variety of matters. But the issue of the Sabbath and what one did on the Sabbath was perhaps the main issue over which they debated and over which they rejected Him. Time and again the matter of the Sabbath was debated.

God had given the Sabbath day to the nation of Israel as a sign of His covenant with them (Ex. 31:12-17; Deut. 5:13-15). It was given as a day of rest and worship, something to benefit them. But the Jews had created a multitude of rules regulating what could or could not be done on the Sabbath day. Practically speaking, their rules were as authoritative as the Law itself. When the disciples of Jesus picked some grain and rubbed it in their hands to remove the chaff, the Pharisees viewed that as work (harvesting and threshing grain) and thus a violation of the Sabbath. Jesus rebuked them and indicated that they misunderstood the whole idea of the Sabbath. The Sabbath was made to benefit man, not to become a burdensome and oppressive part of life (cf. Mark 2:27). Jesus directed their attention back to the Old Testament and to an incident out of the life of David (1 Sam. 21:1-6). On that occasion David was hungry (like the disciples of Jesus) and technically violated the law when he ate bread that had been in the Tabernacle. Only priests were allowed to eat that bread. Normally that was the standard, but in situations of great need, one must not be bound to a sterile legalism. Jesus concluded this encounter by declaring that His authority was greater than any Sabbath regulation (6:5).

Luke then relates another Sabbath incident. We cannot be sure when this one took place. On this occasion Jesus healed a man with a withered hand in the synagogue. Jesus was fully aware that the scribes and Pharisees were waiting for Him to do this in order to accuse Him of working on the Sabbath. In fact, it seems at times that Jesus purposely went out of His way to heal on the Sabbath in order to highlight the oppressive, irrational legalism of the Pharisees. It is hard to believe that they were far more interested in their traditions than in the good being done to this man and others like him. Jesus prefaced His healing of the man with the withered hand by asking the question "Is it lawful to do good on the Sabbath?" (6:9). This question, with its obvious answer, disarmed His opponents. Jesus went ahead and healed the man's hand. There can be no doubt that the issue of the Sabbath was a crucial one in the ministry of Christ. Jesus' "violations" of the Sabbath inspired murderous thoughts in the hearts of His enemies (Mark 3:6; Luke 6:11).

C. HIS DISCIPLES CHOSEN (6:12-49)

The Lord Jesus had many disciples (a disciple is a "learner"), and from this large group of followers He selected twelve. These twelve He named *apostles* (ones "sent with authority"). This was a momentous decision, as Jesus would be spending much of His time and energies training these men. He therefore spent a whole night in prayer to the Father before the selection was made (6:12). The twelve selected as apostles were Simon Peter, Andrew, James, John, Philip, Bartholomew (also called Nathanael), Thomas (also called Didymus), Matthew (also called Levi), James the son of Alphaeus (also called James "the less"), Simon the Zealot (also called Simon the Cananaean), Judas the son of James (also called Thaddaeus), and finally Judas Iscariot. Three other lists of the apostles are found in the New Testament (Matt. 10:2; Mark 3:16; and Acts 1:13). These twelve, with the exception of the traitor, Judas Iscariot, would become part of the foundation for the yet to be established church (Eph. 2:20).

When the Lord Jesus came down from the mountain after the night of prayer and after selecting the twelve apostles, He met with many other disciples of His plus a large number of people who were not disciples but evidenced interest. He healed many who were sick and then addressed the multitude. The message that Jesus gave (6:20-49) is quite similar in content to the Sermon on the Mount (Matt. 5-7). This might be Luke's version of the same sermon, or more likely it is a similar message given at a different time and location. It is not at all surprising to find the Lord teaching similar things to different audiences, since the message He was communicating was needed by all.

Jesus gave some "beatitudes" in this sermon (6:20-26). He spoke of those who are "blessed" ("happy" or "contented") not because of poverty, hunger, or suffering, but because of their relationship with the "Son of Man" (6:22). Even in such extreme conditions, the one who follows Christ can be contented, because of God's sovereignty and the reality of future glory. In contrast to the suffering disciple of Christ is the man who is at home in the present world system (6:24-26). Those who have chosen against the kingdom of God will eventually experience the judgment of God.

In the next section (6:27-36), Jesus gave a radical word about loving others. Disciples are to respond to evil with good and with love. Patience and not retaliation is to be the response of the follower of Christ. These are radical words, and they are also impossible to obey. They drive the serious disciple to his knees as he realizes that without the enablement and the grace of God such commands cannot be kept.

The next section is a warning against trying to take God's prerogative of judgment into our own hands. Disciples are not to sit as judges over other men, but that does not mean that they are to pretend that evil does not exist. Discernment is needed in order to identify the good and the bad fruit (6:43-45). But greater discernment is needed in evaluating our own lives (6:42).

The concluding emphasis is on the need for obedience (6:46-49). It is not enough to be simply exposed to the truth of God. It is essential after having come to understand the will of God, that the disciple of Christ obey. Not to obey is to live a life characterized by self-deception (James 1:22-24). In our present situation with the plethora of tapes, books, and films that make the hearing of spiritual truth a common experience, there is the danger that people will be satisfied with much hearing. (Such was the case in Ezekiel's day; Ezek. 33:30-32.) But the important thing is to obey. Obedience brings stability to the believer's life (6:48), as well as giving clear evidence of his love for Christ (John 14:21).

D. HIS MULTIFACETED MINISTRY (7:1—9:50)

1. His ministry to a Roman centurion (7:1-10). The Lord Jesus finished His sermon and returned to His home base at Capernaum. There He received a request from an unnamed Roman centurion. A centurion was a Roman army officer who had one hundred soldiers under his command. (Luke always portrays these centurions in a favorable light: Luke 23:47; Acts 10:22; 22:26; 23:17; 24:23; 27:43.) The centurion requested that Jesus heal his seriously ill servant, a man who was particularly close to the centurion. He made his request through some of the Jewish elders. This unusual mediating role by the Jewish leaders is explained (7:5). This Roman centurion cared about the conquered people of Israel, and that was evidenced by his financing of a local synagogue building. It should be noted that Matthew also includes this account of the centurion in his gospel but with a different view and emphasis (Matt. 8:5-13). In his account, Matthew has the centurion himself coming to Jesus with the request. Undoubtedly both accounts are accurate, and when they are combined give a much fuller picture of the event. The centurion did send the Jewish elders and then some other friends as Luke says, but then shortly arrived himself as he was overwhelmed with great mental anxiety. (Luke 7:1-8 would be followed by Matt. 8:5*b*-9.)[8] As Jesus approached the house of the centurion, He was told that He did not have to trouble Himself by coming any further. If Jesus would just say the word, healing would take place. The centurion recognized his own unworthiness but also the great authority of the Lord Jesus. Jesus was impressed by the faith of this Gentile and remarked that this kind of faith was not found in Israel. (Matthew emphasizes the centurion's faith even more than Luke does.) The servant of the centurion was healed (7:10).

2. His ministry to a grieving widow (7:11-17). Death was a frightening thing to the Jew. He had just enough knowledge of life beyond the grave to make him afraid but not enough to give him consolation. One pious rabbi cried out on his death bed that it was understandable that he should tremble and weep because he was "about to be led before the King of kings, the Holy One . . . Whose chains are chains for evermore, and Whose sentence of death killeth for ever. . . . And not only so, but there are before me two ways, one to paradise and the other to hell, and I know not which of the two ways I shall have to go."[9] There was no certainty that "absent from the body" is to be present with the Lord (2 Cor. 5:8; Phil. 1:23).

As the Lord Jesus approached the village of Nain in Galilee with His disciples and a multitude of people, He met a funeral procession as it was leaving the town. A young man had died and had left his widowed mother alone in this world. If this

8. Zane Hodges, "The Centurion's Faith in Matthew and Luke," *Bibliotheca Sacra* 121 (October-December 1964): 325-32.
9. Edersheim, *Sketches,* pp. 161-62.

funeral procession was typical it would have been led by women (since Eve was the one who had introduced death into the world); then would come the funeral orator, proclaiming the good deeds of the deceased. After those individuals would come the family (in this case, the mother), followed by the coffin and then the sympathetic multitude.[10]

When Jesus saw the grieving mother, He felt compassion for her (7:13) and approached her, telling her not to cry. He touched the coffin (which normally would have brought defilement according to Mosaic law), and commanded the dead man to get up. Jesus, who is the giver of life, brought physical life to this young man (7:15). The response of the people who observed this was predictable. They feared and they glorified God. They also told everyone about the great prophet, Jesus. Note that they were not saying that Jesus was the "Christ, the Son of the Living God" (Matt. 16:16). That insight comes not by observing miracles, but by divine illumination.

3. His ministry to a doubting prophet (7:18-35). In 3:19-20, Luke recorded the imprisoning of John the Baptist. Now Luke brings John back into the story. John had been in prison for many months. He knew that he had been sent by God to announce the coming Messiah and His kingdom. But something seemingly had gone wrong. He was in prison and no kingdom had come. A horrible thought knifed through John's mind. Had he announced the wrong person? John summoned two of his disciples and sent them to Jesus to ask if He was indeed the Messiah (7:19). These disciples of John asked their question, but Jesus did not verbally respond. Instead, He healed many who were afflicted. Then Jesus spoke to them and told them to report to John the things that they had seen. John's doubts would not have been removed by Jesus' simply saying emphatically, "Yes, of course, I am the Messiah!" By healing the sick, the blind, and the deaf and by preaching God's Word to them, Jesus was fulfilling some very specific messianic proph-

10. Ibid., pp. 169-70.

ecies (such as Isa. 35:5-6; 61:1). The fulfillment of those Scriptures would have had a comforting and encouraging effect on the despondent John. The best way to remove doubts is not by pretending that they do not exist but rather by exposing them to the truth of God.

After the disciples of John left Jesus, He spoke of the greatness of John the Baptist. Jesus asked several rhetorical questions (7:24-25). The first one expected a negative answer. John the Baptist was not like a reed blown around by the wind. He was an unwavering, uncompromising, determined man who knew his job and stuck with it. He was also one who denied himself all earthly comforts in order that his message might be more effective. John was a prophet but was even more than a prophet; he was the one who fulfilled Malachi 3:1. Jesus said that John was the greatest of men (7:28). John announced the long-awaited Messiah of Israel, but John was of the old order. All those who experience the redeeming power of Christ in the New Covenant are greater. (The New Covenant is superior to the Old Covenant; 2 Cor. 3:1-18.) The response to John's ministry had been very different (7:29-30). Jesus declared that the leaders were like foolish children. They were never satisfied. John and Jesus were very different, yet they criticized both vehemently (7:31-35).

4. His ministry to a repentant prostitute (7:36-50). Jesus was invited by a Pharisee to dine at his house. Jesus accepted the invitation because He loved Pharisees too and wanted them to come to saving faith. The Pharisee, whose name was Simon (7:40), had evidently invited Jesus to his house in order to discover if Jesus was indeed a prophet of God, cf. Nicodemus in John 3. These large dinners were typically held in an open room, and often the curious and the poor would gather to observe the rich folks enjoying life. This made access to Jesus a very easy thing.

Luke tells us that a woman with an unsavory reputation (undoubtedly a well-known prostitute) heard that Jesus was dining at Simon's house. She came, entered, humbly approached

Jesus, and anointed His feet with costly perfume and with her tears. It was an act of great love, adoration, and worship. Simon, who knew of this woman's sinful living, concluded that he now knew that Jesus was not really a prophet of God (7:39). Jesus then told Simon one of those simple but incredibly profound stories that characterized His teaching (7:40-42). Jesus concluded by asking Simon a question, the answer to which was obvious. Simon understood that the one who is forgiving the greater debt will most likely be the most grateful. Jesus mildly rebuked Simon for his neglect of common courtesies toward Jesus, who was his guest. Simon's negligence indicated little love, but the woman's actions indicated great love. The key verse is 7:47.

Jesus declared that the woman's sins had been forgiven. Jesus did not say, however, that her sins were forgiven because she loved much. In fact, He taught just the opposite. She realized that she was a great sinner. She was forgiven by Christ and as a result she responded with love and adoration. Undoubtedly the woman had responded to Jesus' message given sometime earlier. On this occasion Jesus informed her that her sins were cleansed. Jesus did not in any way overlook her sinfulness. Her faith had saved her (7:50). Jesus confirmed what had already taken place.

Any sin is a great sin. But the realization of our sinfulness and the realization of our forgiveness by God is one of the most significant factors in developing a godly attitude—an attitude where our love for God is deepened as we appreciate the pit that He pulled us out of; where our ability to forgive others becomes a reality; and where we consciously depend on Him since we understand our sinful capacities. A sense of great forgiveness brings great love and thankfulness.

5. *His ministry supported (8:1-3).* This portion tells us what no other gospel tells us—how Jesus and His disciples lived when they were not being entertained by hospitable people. The common purse, which was kept by Judas Iscariot (John 13:29), was kept supplied by the generosity of certain godly

women, who had themselves been recipients of the Lord's miracles. (Note that though Mary Magdalene had demons cast out of her, nowhere does Scripture suggest that she was immoral, as is often said.)

6. His ministry of teaching (8:4-21). Recorded in this section is one of the most famous parables given by the Lord Jesus, the parable of the sower who scattered his seed on four different kinds of soil. As very large crowds followed Him, Jesus paused, probably out near a cultivated field, and spoke of a farmer who sowed his seed in his field. Jesus said that some of his seed fell on the hardened roadway, some landed on a rocky area, some germinated in a place full of thorns, and other seed fell in good ground and ended up producing a fine crop. All of this was quite familiar to His hearers, but they were somewhat mystified as to the point of the whole lesson. The disciples sensed that there was great significance to what Jesus had just said and questioned Him about the meaning of His parable (8:9). There were indeed crucial issues revealed in this parable, and the disciples were permitted to learn these mysteries (divine secrets which can be understood only by divine illumination).

The key point that opened up this parable was the identification of the seed as the Word of God (8:11). The seed is the same in all four of these situations, yet the results are markedly different. The fruitfulness of the seed depends on the kind of soil on which it falls. The soils represent all of humanity and its response to the Word of God.

The first soil (8:5, 12) clearly pictures the unsaved man. The seed was sown on the roadway and never had an opportunity to germinate, as it was stepped on and then eaten by birds. The seed was initially trampled by man. (This might figuratively look at man's self-centeredness and pride evidenced in his arrogant thoughts, philosophies, and desires.) The role of Satan (the birds) was emphasized by Christ. Satan confuses and darkens the minds of men so that they cannot understand the truth of God (2 Cor. 4:4). It is important to observe that Satan's role of opposing the truth is mentioned only in connection with the first soil (no birds appear in the next three). Only in relation to the first soil was Satan able to keep the seed from producing life.

The second soil (8:6, 13) is the rocky ground, where the seed did germinate but where little else occurred. This is perhaps the most difficult soil to interpret, and there are differences of opinions among Bible commentators. Some see this soil as representing those who only appear to profess Christ as Savior, but in reality remain unsaved.[11] Others believe that life (salvation) has come to the individual, but because of circumstances a living kind of faith dies.[12] A key issue to be decided in order to interpret the difficult second and third soils is the point of how salvation is pictured. Does germination of the seed equal salvation, or does fruitfulness picture salvation? As the Bible interpreter answers this question he will be guided into his interpretation. I prefer the view that the issue of this parable has to do with the real life that comes from the Word of God. The second soil, therefore, represents the individual who truly receives life (salvation) but tragically gives little evidence of it.

> Man, to be sure, was changeable. The God who gifted him was not. And the gift of life, like every other good and perfect gift, had its origin and source in the immutable giver. . . . The living seed remained in the heart. The faith that received it did not.[13]

The third soil (8:7, 14) is the thorny ground where the seed again germinates, but where thorns retard the productivity of the seed. Luke indicates that this third soil did produce fruit, but it was immature, unripe, and thus of no real value (8:14). The choking process was gradual and not sudden. It took place over a period of time. Most spiritual failure is a slow leak and not a sudden blowout. The Word had little room to grow and flourish because of the thorns, which represented worries,

11. H. A. Ironside, *Luke* (Neptune, N. J.: Loizeaux, 1971), p. 245.
12. Zane Hodges, *The Hungry Inherit* (Chicago: Moody, 1972), p. 60.
13. Ibid., pp. 60-61.

riches, and pleasure. *Worries* would be those cares and pressures of daily living that come to engulf a person's life. It could be a job situation, the children, some material possessions, illness, meeting of financial obligations, or a hundred other things. All these matters are to be given to the Lord so that strength and grace may flow from Him to us (Phil. 4:6-8; 1 Pet. 5:6-7). *Riches* have to do with a person's attitude toward wealth and not the size of his bank account. The pursuit of money and material things keeps one from pursuing godliness (1 Tim. 6:9-11). *Pleasures of this life* looks at that illegitimate emphasis, found in so many of our day, which sees personal pleasure as the primary goal and pursuit of life. The ability to enjoy life is a gift from God in its proper place (1 Tim. 4:4-5). The pursuit of pleasure keeps a person from the pursuit of godliness and thus produces emptiness instead of fruitfulness (Eccles. 2:1, 10-11).

It is universally agreed that the fourth soil, the good ground, represents the person who hears the Word of God and is saved, producing a harvest of righteousness and good deeds (8:8, 15). These are genuine believers whose lives are characterized by cleanliness and discipline. Luke simply states that their lives are productive, whereas Matthew and Mark emphasize that even in the fourth soil there are differences in productivity (Matt. 13:23; Mark 4:20). The real question for each of us is, Which soil pictures my life?

After the parable of the seed and soils, Jesus continued with a discussion concerning the Word of God (8:16-18). The Lord told His followers that they were responsible for the knowledge that they had received. They had been "lighted" with the truth, and they were to share the truth of God with others. The person who receives and appropriates the Word into his life has the capacity to receive more truth. But the one who neglects or rejects the truth slowly loses his ability to receive and apply the Word (8:18). People cannot be neutral about the truth of God.

Several times in His ministry the Lord Jesus made clear that the only valid relationship to Him is one that is established by faith in Him and His Word (8:19-21). Mary and Jesus' earthly family had no special claim on Him. (At this time Jesus' brothers were unbelievers, John 7:5.) It was those who heard the Word and obeyed it that had a genuine and vital relationship with Him (8:21).

7. His ministry to the fearful disciples (8:22-25). The Sea of Galilee is well known for the storms that can suddenly and violently come upon it. The mountains around the Sea of Galilee have many ravines that are like funnels through which the wind can rush down with great velocity. One such storm struck when an exhausted Jesus and His disciples were out in a boat (8:23). When the storm hit with such force, they became badly frightened (even though some of them were experienced fishermen). Jesus had fallen asleep, and the disciples woke Him up. (This is one of a number of accounts which illustrate the fact that Jesus was truly human. Here fatigue is seen after days of ministering.) Jesus got up and rebuked the wind and waves, and they immediately calmed down.

The word used for "rebuking" the wind is similar to that used in His casting out demons, which has caused some to speculate that this storm was caused by Satan in an attempt to destroy the Lord Jesus. The disciples were amazed by the sudden calm and evidenced some confusion (8:25). It was difficult to understand how this One who seemed so very human (sleeping because of fatigue) could demonstrate such awesome authority over the natural elements. Jesus rebuked His disciples by asking them, "Where is your faith?" The disciples had faith (all men have a capacity to believe), but the object of their faith on this occasion was not the Lord. They did not necessarily need more faith; they needed to direct their faith properly.

8. His ministry to the demon-possessed (8:26-39). Jesus and His disciples sailed to the eastern shore of Galilee, where He was immediately met by a man who was controlled by demons. He lived in the tombs, and men were generally unable to control Him. When he met Jesus the demons spoke out in fear, declaring that they knew who Jesus was and recognized the authority that He had over them (8:28). When asked by Jesus the demon stated that his name was Legion. A Roman legion consisted of six thousand men, so this name suggests that many demons inhabited the man and that they were an organized force. The demons were afraid that Jesus was going to send them to the abyss (8:31). The abyss is a place where demons can be confined and will be confined during the glorious future kingdom of Christ (Rev. 20:1-3). They knew that the abyss was their place of future confinement but begged to be spared early "retirement" by being permitted to indwell a herd of pigs nearby. Jesus allowed them to enter the swine, and the result was that the swine stampeded into the sea and drowned, much to the distress of those who tended them. Word of this event spread quickly, and the townspeople came out into the countryside to see Jesus and the man who had been freed from the demons. The people observed the man and noted their economic loss and, being afraid, requested Jesus to leave them alone. It must be noted that the demons, not Jesus, destroyed the swine. And furthermore, there is some question as to whether those unclean animals (according to the Old Testament law) should have been there anyhow. The man who had been delivered from the demons wanted to go with Jesus, but Jesus told him to stay and be a testimony of God's grace and power to those in that area. It is obvious that those people needed his witness.

Several things about demons can be learned from this account. First, more than one can possess a human being. Second, they can evidently possess animals as well. Third, they are doctrinally quite orthodox. They know (and believe) that God is in control and that their future is the abyss. Fourth, they have the ability to do some superhuman acts (8:29). And fifth, they are limited in their power. God is greater in power and authority.

9. His ministry to the great and the lowly (8:40-56). When Jesus was about twenty years old and working in the carpenter's shop in Nazareth, a baby girl was born to a prominent religious leader. In the same year a woman was stricken with a physical problem that would plague her for years. Twelve years later their paths crossed one day as Jesus healed the woman and restored the child to life.

Jesus had been rejected by those on the eastern shore of Galilee, but was received warmly by those in the Capernaum area (8:40). One man had especially wanted Jesus to return, and that man was Jairus, an important religious figure in the area. He was an official of the synagogue, which meant he determined the order and conduct of the service, as well as determining who participated at the synagogue. He forced his way through the great crowd to request Jesus to come and heal his only child, a twelve-year-old daughter (8:42).

But before Jesus could do so the woman who had been afflicted for twelve years desperately sought Him as well. She had had a hemorrhage for this length of time and though she had sought to be cured by doctors, no relief had come. (Note that Luke, the physician, does not add what Mark does—that the woman had suffered much at the hands of the doctors. The discharge that the woman had made life miserable for her. Not only did she have to suffer with her physical problems, but there were terrible social and spiritual consequences as well (Lev. 15:25-27). She was ceremonially unclean, and anyone who touched her became unclean.

She was desperate when she came to Jesus. She came to Him with half hope and faith and half superstition ("If I just touch His garments, I shall get well," Mark 5:28). Her faith seemed weak, yet her faith was directed toward One who was strong. The key again is not so much the amount of one's faith but the object of it. She was healed (8:44). She no doubt intended to slip away unnoticed, but Jesus wanted to make this a public matter (8:45). Jesus' purpose was not to embarrass her but to help her. It was important to make this public in order that all might know that she was healed and thus was no longer ceremonially unclean. Also Jesus wanted to reinforce to her the importance of faith (8:48). This may also indicate that spiritual life came to her at this time as well (the phrase used in 8:48 is the same as 7:50, where the town prostitute came to peace and life).

This encounter with the woman must have been a painful but encouraging delay for Jairus—painful because time was so important to his dying daughter but encouraging because he saw once again the power of God flowing through Jesus. But then came the words that Jairus dreaded, "Your daughter has died" (8:49). Those who came with the sad message showed consideration for the Lord Jesus when they said, "Do not trouble the Teacher any more" (8:49). But they showed a lack of faith as well. Jesus told Jairus not to be afraid but rather to put his trust in Him.

Upon arriving at Jairus' house, Jesus took the parents and three disciples (Peter, James, and John) and went in. He informed the mourners who had gathered that the girl only slept. They laughed, and He ministered. The girl was brought back from the dead and reunited with her parents. There has been some discussion by Bible commentators as to whether or not the young girl was actually dead or just in a coma. The fact that all believed her to be dead (which would have been carefully looked into) and the fact that her spirit "returned" (8:55), favors the idea that she had actually died. But in either case, a mighty miracle was performed, giving graphic evidence again that Jesus was the Christ, the Son of the living God.

Faith has been an issue in this chapter (8:25, 48, 50). Faith in the Lord Jesus brought about physical and spiritual healing. It is the same today. Faith in Christ brings life abundant and eternal.

10. His ministry through His disciples (9:1-9). In order to extend His own ministry the Lord Jesus commissioned the twelve to go out preaching and healing. They were to do the same things that He did, only a greater geographical area could be covered. The twelve apostles were empowered to work miracles in order to authenticate the message that they preached. People would be more likely to believe that they were representatives of Messiah if they worked miracles. They were to travel light, accept whatever hospitality was offered to them, and minister with the realization that some would reject them. Luke does not say where the twelve went, but obedient to their commission they went out (9:6). Undoubtedly the Lord designed this as a time for some on-the-job training for these men who would be the foundational element of the church.

One interesting sidelight to this account is the fact that included in this group was the unbelieving traitor, Judas Iscariot. Judas Iscariot preached and healed along with the rest of the twelve, yet he was not a genuine disciple. He illustrates the point that it is possible to be deeply involved in religious activity, deal with the truth of God, and still be an unbeliever. He is probably the classic example of an apostate (one who willfully, knowingly, and deliberately turns from the truth of God).

Included in this section is a further word about Herod Antipas (9:6-9). Herod had heard much about Jesus' ministry but was puzzled as to His identity. Some thought that Jesus was John the Baptist raised from the dead. (Herod had killed John after keeping him imprisoned for about a year.[14]) It is possible that a superstitious Herod Antipas actually believed that John had come back from the dead (9:7). But it is more likely that Herod was speaking more symbolically about Jesus. Herod thought he had ridded himself of a potentially dangerous situation when he had John the Baptist beheaded. But now with Jesus' greater and more influential ministry, Herod was thinking, "Oh no, it is John the Baptist all over again—more problems for me."[15] Luke also states in this section that other people thought that Jesus was Elijah or one of the other prophets. Although they were not clear as to who He was, they were clear on the fact that Jesus was arousing a great deal of interest and enthusiasm among the people.

11. His ministry to the hungry (9:10-17). The feeding of the five thousand men is the only miracle (aside from the resur-

14. Hoehner, p. 171.
15. Ibid., pp. 189-91.

rection) recorded in all four of the gospels.

After the twelve returned from their mission, a private testimony service was held (9:10). But the crowds kept following Jesus and gave Him no rest. He nevertheless gladly preached to them. When it was beginning to get late the disciples suggested that Jesus send the crowds away. The Lord countered that suggestion with one of His own, namely that the disciples feed the multitude before the people departed. The disciples observed their own limited resources and were unsure what to do (9:13). The Lord Jesus took the five loaves (more like biscuits) and two fish the disciples were able to procure and gave thanks for them. He then broke the bread, broke it again, and then again. The amazed disciples watched. The more He broke off the more there was. The hungry crowd ate to the full and when they were satisfied, twelve baskets of food still remained. This event gave them a further lesson in the creative power of the Lord Jesus. It also illustrates for them the truth that He could provide for them. And too, this event of the feeding of the five thousand men was a foreshadowing of the blessing and prosperity of the coming kingdom of the Lord Jesus.

12. His ministry of revelation (9:18-50). Luke begins this section with a very important revelation about the Person of Christ (9:18-27). The Lord Jesus asked His disciples how the crowds viewed Him (9:18). They responded with a variety of answers that revealed that the masses were uncertain about Him but were sure that He was special and was from God (9:19 and 9:7-8). The Lord was not seeking information but was bringing these men to a place where they would have to articulate their position on His Person.

This was a watershed point in their lives. Peter responded for the group by declaring that Jesus was indeed the Christ (Messiah). Matthew gives a fuller account of Peter's statement, including the fact that Jesus was the Son of God (Matt. 16:16). When Peter responded with the truth, Jesus warned them not to reveal this fact (9:21). This seems to be a strange and contradictory command from Christ. It would seem that He would want them to announce this everywhere. But several factors must be remembered. First, Jesus had already given enough signs and evidence for men to come to this conclusion (signs were what Jesus gave to a doubting John the Baptist, 7:18-23). Merely going about and saying that Jesus of Nazareth was the Messiah would not convince them. Second, from what can be gleaned out of the gospels and secular history from the time, the Jews would probably have taken a direct claim to messiahship as a political and military claim. This the Jews had done with others who made claims of messiahship. The people of Israel (including the disciples at that time) did not understand the suffering aspect of the Messiah's life (9:22). Messiah would be a great ruler, but He was also to be the great Savior, and that necessitated His death on the cross. Jesus also noted the ones who would bear the greatest responsibility for His death, the Jewish leadership. The Jewish supreme court (the Great Sanhedrin) would play the key role in His death. (See "Additional Notes" on the *Sanhedrin* at the end of this chapter.)

To follow the Lord Jesus in a time of rejection and suffering was a different matter from following Him in the midst of popular acclaim. Therefore, the Lord Jesus gave some requirements for those who would follow Him—then and now.

First, He stated that a person must desire to be a disciple ("if anyone *wishes* to come after Me" 9:23). There must be a hungering and thirsting after righteousness (Matt. 5:6) on the part of one who would follow Him. No coercion, no scare tactics, just a desire to follow Him was required.

A second requirement for discipleship was the decision to give up the right of self-determination ("deny himself"). This is not speaking of giving up things but rather something more basic. It is a vow to give the control of life to Christ. It is a decisive, rational, calculated choice, not an emotional, unthinking response. The concept of voluntary slavery seems to be in view here (Deut. 15:12-17).

The third requirement is that one must daily identify with Christ ("take up his cross daily and follow Me"). This is a voluntary action, and it is a daily experience. The cross pictures the giving up of life for Christ (2 Cor. 4:7, 10-11). A disciple identifies himself with Christ by obeying Him, by living a biblical life-style. Jesus then told of the consequences of following or not following Him (9:24-26). To so give one's life to Christ and submit to His control would bring meaning and blessing. Conversely, the person who chose to live for himself and his own pleasure and gain would have an empty and meaningless life. Jesus spoke of those who believed in Him but were ashamed to let that be known. Such a way of life will have consequences when the Lord returns, which will be a time of rewarding for His followers.

The next section also has to do with the Person of Christ, as He is revealed in a unique way at the transfiguration (9:28-36). Luke's account of the transfiguration is the most complete in the gospels. Jesus took three of the disciples (Peter, James, and John) up on a mountain with Him to pray. Mt. Hermon, located near Caesarea-Philippi, is the most likely spot for this event. While upon the mountain, Jesus' appearance changed, and His clothing became white and gleaming (9:29). Two men, identified as Moses and Elijah, appeared and spoke with Jesus about the events that were about to take place in Jerusalem—His death and resurrection. The disciples missed some of this event because they were asleep, but they did not miss the voice from heaven. God spoke commanding them to listen to His Son (9:35). Soon the supernatural events were over, and Jesus told them not to speak of these things for a period of time (Matt. 17:9; 2 Pet. 1:16-18).

Why was the glory of the Lord Jesus Christ allowed to be revealed for a moment up on the mountain? Why did the Father speak so men could hear? Why did Moses and Elijah come and discuss Jesus' coming sacrifice? The unique event of the transfiguration occurred at a time when Jesus was being rejected by men, and it was, therefore, necessary. First, it fulfilled the Lord's statement that some with Him would not die until they saw Him as He would be in His kingdom (9:27). Second, it was essential to show that God approved of Jesus even though man might reject Him. Third, it was an encouragement to Christ as He faced suffering and death. This was undoubtedly the role of Moses and Elijah. Fourth, the transfiguration event was an encouragement to these disciples who had given up everything to follow Jesus.

In the last part of this section (9:37-50), Luke briefly gives several incidents that reveal more of His Person and power. In the first incident a father pleaded with Jesus on behalf of his demon-controlled son (9:37-45). Jesus' disciples had been unable to cast out the demon, but Jesus simply rebuked the demon and it departed. The disciples were told that the reason for their failure was unbelief and a lack of prayer (Matt. 17:20 adds this detail to the account given by Luke). Perhaps it should be observed here that the disciples in this setting represent an all too common problem—prayerless ministry.

A second incident in this section revolves around an ongoing problem with the disciples, that of pride (9:46-48). The disciples on several occasions argued over who would be greatest in the kingdom. Jesus would deal with this later on.

A third incident involved James and John's rebuking of an exorcist who was not one of Jesus' disciples (9:49-50). Jesus is not suggesting compromise here but does rebuke them for their bigoted spirit.

Additional Notes

THE SYNAGOGUE

The word *synagogue* means a "gathering of people" or a "congregation." It was a place where the Jews gathered to study the Scriptures and to worship God.

With the destruction of the Jerusalem Temple in 586 B.C. at the hands of the Babylonians, the Jews no longer had a place to worship. They were taken to Babylon away from their homeland. The synagogue can be traced back to this Babylonian captivity, when Jews, encouraged and led by Ezekiel, met for study and worship (Ezek. 8:1; 20:1-3). The synagogue was an important factor in keeping the displaced Jews from lapsing into heathenism. Gradually it became customary, after the Jews' return from exile, for local meeting places to be established for study and worship. During the intertestament period, synagogues multiplied both in and out of Palestine.[16]

At the time of Christ, synagogues could be found everywhere throughout the land. It was said by some rabbis that, when Jerusalem was destroyed by the Romans in A.D. 70, there were more than 450 synagogues in Jerusalem alone. And although that may be an exaggeration, it does reveal how numerous they were in Christ's day. It took ten pious men to start one, so even the smaller towns could have a synagogue. It would not be difficult to find the synagogue upon entering a town. It was located on the highest point of ground in the city, or if not, it had a spire on top, which would make it the highest building in town. This was done to symbolize that the functions of the synagogue were the most important thing possible for the people to engage in. Also, this supposedly fulfilled Isaiah 2:2 where the house of the Lord would be established on the chief of the mountains and raised above the high hills. (If the synagogue was lower than other buildings it was thought to be in danger of destruction.)[17]

The services of the synagogue enjoyed great freedom, and

16. Edersheim, *Life and Times,* 1:432-34.
17. Edersheim, *Sketches,* pp. 250-64.

any competent Israelite could participate even if he was just visiting (such as Jesus or Paul). There was order to the services—portions of the Law and Prophets were read systematically during the year. Each synagogue had a ruler whose duty it was to oversee the services and insure order. The scrolls were central to the synagogue and were handled with great care. When used in a service, the scrolls were handled by an "attendant" and were immediately put back into their proper place when the reading of them concluded (Luke 4:20). In the synagogue services men and women were separate from one another, and only the men participated in the services.

The synagogue also became an important place for the training of Jewish boys in the faith of Judaism (girls were taught at home). All boys had the opportunity of synagogue training until about the age of twelve.

The synagogue was then part of the heart and core of Jewish life in the days of Christ. Although the Temple existed then, the synagogue remained the central place in the life of the average Jew, as he studied the Scriptures and worshiped God.

THE PHARISEES

The name *Pharisee* comes from a Hebrew word that means "to separate," and so the Pharisees were referred to as the separated ones.[18] From the time of the Jews' return from the Babylonian captivity through the intertestament period, a movement for purity for the things of the Lord Jehovah grew. There came into existence in Judaism a movement that was determined to be free from pagan influences. The Syrian king Antiochus Epiphanes (175 B.C.) gave great momentum to this separatist movement when he tried to force heathen practices on the Jewish people. From about 125 B.C. the distinct party of the Pharisees can be found in the Jewish society,.

The Pharisees believed strongly in a separation from the ways and practices of the Gentiles. And they taught, in great detail, what was involved in that separation. For example,

18. Norval Geldenhuys, *Commentary on the Gospel of Luke* (Grand Rapids: Eerdmans, 1966), p. 189.

> Three days before a heathen festival all transactions with Gentiles were forbidden, so as to afford them neither direct nor indirect help towards their rites; and this prohibition extended even to private festivities. . . . It was unlawful for Jewish workmen to assist in anything that might be subservient either to heathen worship or heathen rule, including in the latter the erection of court-houses and similar buildings. . . . Milk drawn from a cow by heathen hands, bread and oil prepared by them, might indeed be sold to strangers, but not used by Israelites. If a heathen were invited to a Jewish house, he might not be left alone in the room, else every article of food or drink on the table was henceforth to be regarded as unclean. If cooking utensils were bought of them, they had to be purified by fire or by water; knives to be ground anew, spits to be made red-hot before use, etc.[19]

This quotation reveals the prevailing attitude of the Pharisees in Christ's day.

The Pharisees had an unbending loyalty to the Scriptures and desired to live strictly by the law. In their desire to make the law workable in practical life, they developed a system of regulations and traditions, which by the time of Christ had become a terrible burden on the people. The Pharisees promoted these traditions to a place of equal or (practically speaking) greater importance than the written law. They became proud of their separation and knowledge and viewed themselves as superior to the rest of society. It was their pride, self-righteousness, and violation of the spirit of the law that brought about the harsh condemnations of them by the Lord Jesus. It should be added, however, that their zeal for the law kept the messianic hope burning brightly in Israel in those days of Roman rule.

The actual number of Pharisees in the days of Christ was

19. Edersheim, *Sketches,* pp. 26-28.

around six thousand.[20] They were not a very large group, but still they wielded tremendous power in Israel because they had the wholehearted support of the people.

> We see, therefore, that doubtless the Pharisees were the people's party; they represented the common people as opposed to the aristocracy on both religious and social matters. Their much respected piety and their social leanings towards suppressing differences of class, gained them the people's support and assured them, step by step, of the victory. There is something very impressive about the way in which the people unreservedly followed the Pharisees . . . as a whole the people looked to the Pharisees, in their voluntary commitment to works of supererogation, as models of piety, and as embodiments of the ideal life which the scribes, these men of divine and secret knowledge, had set before them. It was an act of unparalleled risk which Jesus performed when, from the full power of his consciousness of sovereignty, he openly and fearlessly called these men to repentance, and this act brought him to the cross.[21]

There were several different groups within the pharisaic community, and they did differ among themselves on various points of the law. Entrance into the ranks of the Pharisees was preceded by a period of probation, from one month to a year. During this time the personal piety and zeal of the candidate was observed. Tithing, fasting, and separation from uncleaness were basic matters to be observed. Once within the ranks of pharisaism increasingly strict vows could be taken.

THE SCRIBES

The scribes were not a party as were the Pharisees but were rather a class of Israelites. They were well-educated persons

20. Joachim Jeremias, *Jerusalem in the Time of Jesus* (Philadelphia: Fortress, 1969), p. 252.
21. Ibid., pp. 266-67.

whose job it was to teach and interpret the law. They are also referred to in the gospels as the "doctors of the law" and the "lawyers." They not only taught the law but were responsible to prosecute those who broke the law (this is what Saul of Tarsus was doing when he was prosecuting the Christians). Evidence points to the fact that the great majority of the scribes belonged to the party of the Pharisees, and thus the close association in the gospel record between the scribes and the Pharisees. It must be noted that whereas most scribes were Pharisees, most Pharisees were not scribes. It would be correct to say that in the days of Christ, the most influential members of the pharisaic party were the scribes.[22]

THE SANHEDRIN

The word *sanhedrin* (which was derived from the Greek and given a Hebraic form) is rather broad in its meaning. Basically it has the idea of a council or a governing body, but it can also include the idea of a court.[23] The Great Sanhedrin was the national council of the Jews (something like a Jewish "supreme court"). It was made up of seventy-one members; the high priest was the president. The Sanhedrin met in Jerusalem in the confines of the Temple. Although the idea of a representative council can be found in the time of Ezra, the sanhedrin of the New Testament era traces its organization to about the time of John Hyrcanus (135 B.C.), the days of Jewish independence in the intertestament period.

There were numerous small sanhedrins, or councils, in the towns throughout Judea and Galilee, but these were limited in power and influence as they dealt with local matters. The Great Sanhedrin, however, had great power and involved itself in both religious and civil matters. This power, of course, was limited because of the domination of Rome. (The sanhedrin was stripped of a great deal of power, including that of capital

22. Ibid., p. 254.
23. F. F. Bruce, *New Testament History* (New York: Doubleday, 1971), p. 77.

punishment, in the days of Herod the Great.)[24] But the Romans did allow the sanhedrin extensive authority in Jewish internal affairs.

It was the Great Sanhedrin that found itself in conflict with the Lord Jesus (John 9:1-41). They attempted to arrest Him on several occasions (e.g., John 7:32); they desired to kill Him (e.g., Luke 22:2); they participated in His arrest (Mark 14:43); they broke their own laws and code of ethics in their trial of Him (e.g., Matt. 26:59; 27:41); and they are held accountable by Scripture for their actions (Acts 2:23, 36; 3:13).

The Great Sanhedrin is identified by a variety of designations in the gospels and the book of Acts. It is sometimes referred to as the "council" (Matt. 26:59; Acts 4:15), the "council of elders' (Acts 22:5), and the "senate" (Acts 5:21). But it is mainly identified in the New Testament by its component elements, such as "chief priests and pharisees," "chief priests, elders, and scribes," or the rulers, elders, and scribes.[25] The "elders" were men from the leading families in Judaism, many of whom would trace their roots back to the key families of Ezra's day. The "chief priests" were actually priests of higher rank and authority than the ordinary priest.[26] And the Pharisees (discussed previously) were sometimes referred to as the scribes, showing the close association between these two. Luke speaks of the Great Sanhedrin, using its component elements, in 9:22; 19:47; 20:19; 22:2 and 22:66.

24. Emil Schurer, *A History of the Jewish People in the Time of Jesus* (New York: Schocken, 1961), pp. 109-10).
25. Werner Forster, *Palestinian Judaism in New Testament Times* (London: Oliver and Boyd, 1964), p. 124.
26. Jeremias, pp. 178-79.

3

THE MINISTRY OF JESUS THE SON OF MAN IN TIMES OF REJECTION

(LUKE 9:51—19:27)

At this point in Luke's gospel the Lord Jesus left Galilee, with Capernaum as a center, and journeyed to Jerusalem. On a number of occasions, Luke specifically states that Jesus was headed toward Jerusalem (9:51, 53; 13:22, 33; 17:11; 18:31; 19:11, 28). The exact itinerary of the journey is not clear as Luke is not precise in many details of chronology and location. But Luke is clear that from the time Jesus left Galilee, His sufferings and the cross were central in His thinking. The extent of time from His departure out of Galilee to the events of the Passion Week in Jerusalem were probably about three or four months. (From the limited accounts in Matthew and Mark it seems as though this last journey took a couple of weeks only.) This section of Luke includes His ministry in Perea (that province east of the Jordan River), as well as incidents from Samaria and Bethany.

This section is one of Luke's most significant contributions to our knowledge of the ministry of Christ. John has some material from this time in Christ's life, but it is Luke that gives so many rich details not found in the other three gospels. In this section, Luke deals largely with the teachings of Christ, just as he emphasized the works of Christ in the previous portion. Many parables and teachings of Christ are found here and nowhere else, such as those priceless stories of the Prodigal Son and the parable of the Good Samaritan.

The chart, figure 3.1, illustrates something of the emphasis and contribution of Luke to our understanding of the ministry of Christ.

EMPHASIS IN LUKE'S GOSPEL

CHAPTERS IN LUKE	1:1—2:52	3:1—9:50	9:51—19:27	19:28—24:53
TIME INVOLVED	About 30 Years	3 Years	3-4 Months	8 Days

Fig. 3.1

A. HIS FINAL JOURNEY TO JERUSALEM (9:51-62)

1. The rejection by the Samaritans (9:51-56). Encouraged and challenged by the event of the transfiguration, Jesus was ready to go to Jerusalem. The time for His "ascension" had come (9:51). This is the only place in the New Testament where this noun form is found. It is looking at Jesus' death, resurrection, and ascension. Jesus chose to travel through Samaria, on His way from Galilee to Jerusalem, and He sent messengers ahead to prepare for His stay in a Samaritan village (9:52). When the Samaritans realized that Jesus was not coming to them, but rather His purpose was simply to stop there on His way to Jerusalem, they wanted nothing to do with Him. This rejection of Jesus brought a reaction from James and John. Probably remembering the time when the prophet Elijah (whom they had just seen on the mount of transfiguration) called down fire from heaven when the Lord Jehovah was rejected (2 Kings 1:9-11), these disciples suggested the same action for the Samaritans. The Lord rebuked this attitude of antagonism and simply went to another village, where presumably He was accepted.

2. The responses of potential disciples (9:57-62). In this brief section something more about true discipleship is revealed as three situations are brought together by Luke. These three men illustrate those who fail to fulfill the requirements given for discipleship (9:23-25). The first individual volunteered to go with Jesus anywhere that He went (9:57-58). This man (who was evidently a scribe, Matt. 8:19) really did not understand what it meant to follow Christ. He evidently did not realize the personal sacrifice and the hardship involved. It was not a life of glory to follow one who did not even have a place to lay His head.

The second person was approached by Jesus but said that he needed to go and bury his father (9:59-60). Jesus responded by saying that the dead (spiritually) can bury their own dead. This statement seems harsh, but evidently the man's statement reflected that his priorities were wrong. Most likely the man's father was ill, but had not died (or perhaps his father was quite aged). The man's loyalty to his father was greater than his loyalty to Christ.

The third man also volunteered himself to Jesus but with the reservation that he had to go home and say good-bye (9:61-62). On the surface this seems to be reasonable. But the rebuke by Jesus reveals that there was some reluctance on the man's part. He had not denied himself (9:23) or counted the cost of discipleship (14:33). He wanted conditional discipleship, but Jesus made clear that a person is not useful ("fit") for His service if he has divided loyalties.

B. HIS INSTRUCTION IN VIEW OF HIS REJECTION (10:1—19:27)

1. The sending out of the seventy to minister (10:1-24). As the Lord's ministry rapidly drew to a close, there were still many towns and villages that He had not ministered in. As a result of this need, Jesus sent out seventy of His disciples, in groups of two, to preach and to heal. Jesus would Himself come to these places later, but this initial contact gave these towns an opportunity to be prepared for the Lord's personal coming. These seventy were given power to authenticate their message with miracles (10:9).

As Jesus prepared to send them out He instructed them about some of the realities in serving Him. There is real danger in the service of Christ (10:3; 2 Cor. 4:5-11); there is an urgency in His service with the result that a servant cannot become entangled in the issues of life (10:4; 2 Tim. 2:4); and there must be the realization that not everyone will be responsive to the truth (10:5-11). Jesus told them that men are responsible for the truth that is given to them, and those who have received much revelation have the greater responsibility to respond to that revelation (10:13-16). Those cities around the Sea of Galilee had received much revelation, in actual teachings as well as in miracles. Yet they had not responded in belief, and in the day of judgment their accountability before God would be far greater than even some notably sinful cities.

The seventy disciples went out and probably came back to a prearranged place at a prearranged time. They were delighted that their ministry evidenced the blessing and power of God. They had even been victorious over the demons. Jesus also rejoiced in that fact, viewing Satan as a defeated enemy (10:18). But Jesus exhorted them to rejoice in their permanent status as God's children and not in their accomplishments, even if those demonstrated the blessing of God. Our ground of joy is to be our unchanging relationship with Christ and not our temporary accomplishments.

This section concludes with the Lord Jesus' giving praise to the Father for the understanding given to those who are childlike (as opposed to those who are arrogant). Divine illumination is absolutely essential if the things of God are to be understood by any human (see 1 Cor. 1:20-24; 2:10-13). The contrast in the Scriptures is not between the educated and the uneducated but between those who humbly receive God's truth and those who arrogantly reject God's Word as foolishness. Jesus encouraged His disciples by informing them that they were understanding things long concealed (Luke 24:44-45; 1 Pet. 1:10-12).

2. *The parable of the Good Samaritan (10:25-37).* A question that Jesus evidently was asked on a number of occasions had to do with the issue of the reception of eternal life. On this

occasion, Jesus had been teaching a group that was seated when a lawyer (scribe) stood up and asked a question. Luke immediately lets us know that the lawyer's motive was impure (10:25). He either wanted to discredit Jesus or perhaps to test His ability as a teacher. He wanted to know what Jesus thought about the obtaining of eternal life.

Jesus was never content to have theoretical discussions and so forced the lawyer back to the only authoritative source for answering such questions, the law of God. The lawyer came up with the correct answer (10:27), but Jesus perceived that the lawyer had never really seen himself clearly in the mirror of the Law of God. If a person could love God totally and consistently and also love others, then eternal life could be obtained. But no one can do that. The law was given to reveal the perfection of God and, as a result, the sinfulness of man (Rom. 3:19-24; Gal. 3:10-13). Jesus told the lawyer to be loving God always and his neighbor as well. Jesus was attempting to get this scholar to open his eyes and really see his situation.

The lawyer caught the implication of Jesus' statement and immediately tried to justify himself (10:29). He asked a second question, "Who is my neighbor?" It must be noted that the parable of the Good Samaritan was answering the second question, "Who is my neighbor?" and not the first question, "What shall I do to inherit eternal life?" The parable of the Good Samaritan is not teaching us that by doing good to others we receive eternal life.

The road from Jerusalem to Jericho descended some 3,000 feet over its seventeen-mile length. It went through a desolate wilderness area and was, as a result, infested with robbers. A man (presumably a Jew) journeyed down the road and was robbed, beaten, and left for dead. A priest came by and observed this apparently dead man. Wishing to avoid any possibility of defilement (Lev. 21:1), he kept going. Similarly a Levite (perhaps going up to serve God in the Temple at Jerusalem) saw the beaten man and simply avoided him. A third individual, who was a Samaritan, came along next and he too observed the man's condition. He did what he could in caring for his wounds, put the beaten man on his own animal (thus walking himself), and brought him to an inn where the wounded man could recuperate. The Samaritan gave money to the innkeeper (an amount that may have taken care of him for two to three months), and promised that if that amount was insufficient he would pay the rest when he came through Jericho the next time.

Jesus then asked the lawyer a question that had an obvious answer (10:36). The lawyer could not avoid the answer but did avoid using the name *Samaritan* in his answer. It was clear that any person who crossed his path in life and had need was to be classified as a neighbor. The lawyer could not avoid the implications of the Lord's statement. Jesus then exhorted him to be like the Samaritan (see Titus 2:14; 3:14; James 2:14-19).

3. Mary and Martha, worship and service (10:38-42). The next event recorded by Luke took place in the home of Martha and Mary. John 11:1 locates this event in Bethany. Martha was probably the older of the two, since it is said that this episode took place in her home (10:38). Jesus and a unspecified number of followers arrived in Bethany, and Martha, motivated undoubtedly by generosity, hospitality, and love for the Lord, wanted to make it a special time for Him. She became deeply involved in her preparations, while her sister Mary sat and listened to Jesus teach. The task was evidently too much for Martha, and she approached the Lord Jesus to persuade Him to get Mary to help her. There is an element of reproach for Mary and the Lord in her statement (10:40). The harmony between Martha and the others was broken. Jesus' response to Martha was both tender and instructive. Jesus noted that Martha was pulled in several directions at once and her service was characterized by anxiety and stress. He noted that life has very few real necessities, but one of those is communion with Him. Worship is not an option for quality living but is a cornerstone for healthy, spiritual living. Mary was commended for her wise choice.

Jesus was not teaching that active service is unimportant (the parable of the Good Samaritan revealed that). Jesus was teaching that communion with Him is the primary concern. Personal worship and active service are both needed. But service done with great anxiety and the breaking of harmony between people is not to be commended. Years later the Ephesian church would be praised by Christ for its active service but warned that its lack of love for Christ would have disastrous results (Rev. 2:1-7).

4. Instruction on prayer (11:1-13). The prayer life of the Lord Jesus greatly impressed His disciples. There was something about His praying that was noticeably different. There was a quality, a realism, a productivity about His praying that created a need in the hearts of the disciples. Undoubtedly these men had often prayed, but now they asked Him to teach them to pray, and not just to say prayers. Jesus responded by giving them the necessary ingredients for effective prayer, followed by a brief parable with application. Jesus gave the basic components of prayer (11:2-4), but He did not give these to be prayed in a formal, ritualistic way. (In Acts, the church is never seen praying "the Lord's prayer.")

He gave six basic elements of genuine, productive prayer. First, the relationship with God must be real ("Father"). Prayer is to be based on a relationship that has come about because of regeneration and continues through sanctification. A second element is that of worship ("hallowed be Thy name"). Praise to God for who He is and what He has done gives a proper perspective on everything in life (cf. Phil. 4:6; Col. 4:2). Third, as believers pray, they must desire above all else God's will ("Thy kingdom come"). Fourth, His people are to make requests of Him, recognizing their utter dependence on Him ("Give us each day our daily bread"). A fifth element is the frank confession of sin ("and forgive us our sins"). And sixth, the believer must recognize his weakness and absolute dependency on God ("and lead us not into temptation").

After giving these basic components for effective prayer, Jesus then told a story that emphasized the necessity of persistence in prayer. Jesus stated that a man was caught in an unfortunate position late one night when an unexpected guest arrived at an unexpected hour. The law of hospitality was sacred to the Jews, and the man felt constrained to feed his guest even though his cupboard was empty. He went to his neighbor and pounded on his door and made request for some bread to feed his guest. His request was turned down. The man could have given up and been embarrassed, or he could have continued pounding on his neighbor's door. He chose to be persistent with the result that he got the bread he requested. Jesus then encouraged His disciples to be persistent and promised that persistence in prayer would bear results (11:10).

If the teaching of Christ stopped at this point, one might conclude that God must be persuaded to give good things to His followers and that He is somewhat tightfisted. Jesus made clear however, that God is very generous and loves to give (11:11-13). But if God is generous, then why do His followers have to persist in prayer? The answer comes when the two parts of Jesus' teaching on prayer are joined together. More often than not the prayers of God's people do not align themselves with the pattern given by Christ. Perhaps sin has not really been dealt with in the believer's life, or perhaps what he wants is his own will, and in fact, the will of God is not the greatest desire of his heart. When prayer is not answered, the follower of Christ is to analyze his prayers in light of Christ's inspired pattern of prayer. Does his praying follow the pattern given by the Lord? Time before the Lord will often reveal the deficiency. (Of course, the Word of God is a critical element in any self-evaluation.)

5. The rejection of Jesus by the leaders of Israel (11:14-54). As the Lord worked His miracles, it became quite evident that they were truly supernatural. The leadership of Israel was faced with a dilemma. If they conceded that the miracles were from God, then they should bow before the Lord Jesus and acknowledge that He was God's Messiah for Israel. But their pride restrained them from doing this, so they were forced to explain His mighty works as originating with Satan. Attributing the works of Christ to Satan became the standard answer of the leaders for the miracles of the Lord Jesus. About one year prior to this event recorded by Luke, a similar incident took place that caused the ministry of Jesus to change radically (Matt. 12:22-37). The accounts in Luke and Matthew are distinct because: (1) Luke appears to place this event in Judea whereas Matthew's is in Galilee; (2) Luke states that the man healed in this account was dumb, while Matthew's healing is of one who is blind and dumb (Luke, the physician, would surely have mentioned blindness if this had been the man's condition); and (3) the events following are quite different, with Luke telling of a breakfast with a Pharisee and Matthew telling of the initiation of parabolic teaching.[1]

The significance of this rejection of Christ by the leaders of Israel must be understood. These men were not simply ordinary men with a differing religious philosophy. These men were the most influential men in Israel and were men who held the places of great authority and responsibility. They sat in "Moses' seat" (Matt. 23:2) as Jesus later reminded His disciples. They were in a God-ordained position of authority, and as the leaders went, so would go the people. The utter seriousness of this charge against Jesus is analyzed well by the following statement.

> In this charge the vindictive opposition of the religious rulers of Israel reached a new plateau beyond which it could not go. It was bad enough to regard Him as a religious enthusiast "beside Himself," or to put Him on a level with earlier prophets (Matt. 16:13-14), or to reject Him as a law-breaking imposter (John 5:16), or even the unfortunate victim of demon-possession. But to admit the genuineness of His miracles, which had been foretold in their own Scriptures, and then to charge Him with hav-

1. Robert L. Thomas and Stanley N. Gundry, *A Harmony of the Gospels* (Chicago: Moody, 1978), p. 139.

> ing done these things by the powers of hell, thus ascribing wickedness to their own incarnate Messiah—this was something new and terrible among the many sins of the chosen nation. And the charge provoked from the Son of God an ultimatum of such unparalleled severity that it stands alone in the gospel records as an appropriate witness to the awful possibilities of human sin in the face of the light of God's grace.[2]

Jesus responded to this charge with three lines of argumentation.

First, Jesus pointed out how illogical they were when they said that He cast out demons in the power of Satan. He explained that division within a unit will always destroy it, whether that unit be a household or a kingdom (11:17-18). Jesus had literally cast out thousands of demons, and if He did that in Satan's power then there was civil war within Satan's kingdom and it would fall. Satan is not in the process of destroying himself.

Second, Jesus noted that the religious leaders were inconsistent. They had always attributed exorcisms to God, that is, until Jesus came along (11:19-20). All the Jews viewed exorcism as a gift from God and all would immediately observe the inconsistency in the statement of the leaders.

Third, Jesus used the illustration of the house of a strong man. He noted that one entering the house to rob it must have greater power than the one who defends it. Christ's power is greater than the power of demons; therefore, His power is from God (11:21-22).

Next Jesus emphasized the impossibility of neutrality in spiritual matters (11:23), which He then illustrated using the picture of a demon and a man (11:24-26). No man or nation (Israel) can be neutral; either they are walking in the light, or they are walking in the darkness.

2. Alva J. McClain, *The Greatness of the Kingdom* (Chicago: Moody, 1968), p. 313.

At this point the Lord's rebuttal to the charge of the leaders was interrupted by a woman in the crowd. The woman exclaimed how wonderful it would be to have a son like Jesus and that Mary was indeed blessed (11:27). Jesus did not deny the validity of her statement, but used it to make a more significant point. He noted that it is not a physical relationship to Him that is important, but rather a spiritual one. Very few would ever be physically related to the Lord Jesus, but a more meaningful relationship was open to all who would obey the Word of God. This is a key point in Christ's thinking and teaching.

It is essential to respond to the truth of God. This Israel had not done. Israel sought for more and more signs to verify that Jesus was the Messiah, but no more signs would be given, except for the great sign of the resurrection of Christ (11:26, 29). Israel had been given so much truth and yet remained in unbelief. In the day of judgment the heathen would be witnesses against Israel (11:30-32). Jesus then explained that the purpose of light (God's truth) is to reveal and keep a man from falling. If a man is blind, however, then the light does no good. Israel by choice was turning from the light and as a result remained in darkness spiritually.

After teaching the crowds Jesus was invited to lunch with a Pharisee (11:37). The Pharisee was amazed that Jesus did not ceremonially cleanse Himself before eating. (The issue was not that Jesus' hands were dirty, but rather that He did not follow their meticulous traditions of ceremonial washings.) The Pharisee evidently censored the Lord and elicited a scathing denunciation from Him. He censored their externalism (11:39-41), lack of love and mercy (11:42), pride (11:43), and their resulting uncleaness (11:44). Contact with a tomb made one ceremonially unclean, and when Jesus called the Pharisees concealed tombs, He was saying that they were a hidden source of spiritual defilement.

Some lawyers resented Jesus' declaration, and that brought forth from Christ an even greater denunciation. Jesus pointed out the terrible sinfulness of that generation. Their ancestors had killed God's prophets, and now they would kill the One the prophets spoke about. Jesus declared that this generation now living would be severely judged for its sin (11:51). (This would be fulfilled in the Roman wars of A.D. 66-73, when hundreds of thousands of Jews died in a bloody holocaust.)

This bold, powerful rebuke of the prideful leaders of Israel before the people brought a reaction from the leaders. With renewed hostility they attempted to catch Him in His teachings, so that they could bring charges against Him.

6. Instruction concerning hypocrisy (12:1-12). Jesus' public censoring of the religious leaders of Israel and their counter-attack attracted thousands of people. Even with the huge crowd that was present, Jesus focused His attention on His disciples, those that had committed themselves to Him (12:1). He warned them to watch out for the leaven of the Pharisees, which He identified as hypocrisy. The illustration of leaven would have been quite familiar to the listeners. A little yeast (leaven) would gradually but relentlessly permeate a large lump of bread dough. It is used in the Bible to picture evil and the relentless permeation of that evil. The word *hypocrite* means to play a part, be an actor, or role play. It was used of those who were actors on the stage.

Jesus alerted His followers to the subtle but devastating sin of spiritual role playing—pretending to be something that one is not. The Pharisees appeared to be the most righteous and orthodox of men, yet many of them were the wickedest and most corrupt of men in God's eyes. Jesus desired personal integrity for His disciples and warned them that hypocrisy comes on slowly, gradually, and can eventually permeate the entire life of an individual. Jesus then explained that the hypocrite is always involved in covering things up. Yet, this is very shortsighted, since everything will one day be open and revealed—usually in this life, but definitely at the time of judgment (12:2-3).

The major reason for hypocrisy is the fear of man. Fear of what people might say or think causes a person to play a part. Yet, Jesus explained that only God is to be feared (12:4-5). It is God who has the power over physical life and eternal life. It is noteworthy that the Bible teaches that this reverence for God will liberate man from the fear of man and will keep him from sinful living (Prov. 16:6). The fear of God is a missing dimension in the lives of many believers today.[3]

Jesus then encouraged His disciples with the truth that this God they are to reverence deeply cares about them (12:6-7). Our open and honest acknowledgement of Christ is seen as the opposite of hypocrisy. To deny Christ, by word or action. evidences a fear of man and thus a hypocritical life. Even in the most severe times (when the fear of man would be the greatest), the believer is promised help in this time of need (12:12).

7. *Instruction concerning covetousness (12:13-34).* Once again in His public teaching the Lord Jesus was interrupted by someone in the crowd. A man (obviously not too interested in the subject of hypocrisy) asked the Lord Jesus to intervene on his behalf and settle the matter of his inheritance. The man probably had been cheated by his brother and was calling for the intervention of a rabbi to deal with the matter (this was commonly done). Jesus was far less concerned with the legal decision, however, than He was with the heart attitude toward material possessions. Jesus warned the man and all who were listening to be alert and guard themselves against materialism (12:15). He followed this warning with the parable of the rich man (12:16-21). It is worth noting that eleven times the rich man used the first person; he was obviously a very self-centered man (perhaps like the man who interrupted Jesus). The rich man was not concerned with using his wealth wisely, and he did not have God's view of wealth (12:19, 21). He was a fool (12:20) and assumed that since he had wealth in abundance he had control of his life. He did not see his wealth as a blessing from God to be used to His glory. Jesus concluded that all who hoard their wealth and do not invest it in that which counts for eternity are fools (see discussion of Luke 16:1-13).

3. A. W. Tozer, *The Knowledge of the Holy* (New York: Harper and Row, 1961), pp. 6-12.

Jesus then focused His attention back on His disciples (12:22-34). He repeatedly encouraged them not to worry about money and material possessions (12:22, 25, 26, 29). The key to combating materialism and covetousness, Jesus taught, is to grow in trust and confidence in our heavenly Father and to come to understand that He does care for His children. Nothing is accomplished through worry, but much comes through trusting the Father. Jesus reminded them that God provides and cares for the insignificant things in this world, and He certainly will care for them (12:27-28). Jesus instructed them that the priority of life is not to accumulate material possessions (like the unsaved man does, 12:30), but to use time and energy to serve and please Him. Jesus concluded this discussion by encouraging the disciples to remember that God is a giver (12:32) and to release their grip on their material possessions and be ready to use them. (Jesus is not calling for a form of socialism here; many in the New Testament owned houses, boats, animals, and so on, and were never condemned by Christ for that ownership).

8. Instruction concerning watchfulness (12:35-41). Using the imagery of a wedding feast, Jesus encouraged His servants to be ready at all times for His return. Wedding feasts were of an undetermined length, and a man might return at any time day or night (since these feasts went for days it would be less than certain when he would come home). The apostle Paul reminded Christians that there is a special reward for those who "love His appearing" (2 Tim. 4:8). Very often Christians theologically believe that Jesus can return at any moment, but their lifestyles give evidence that they really do not believe that such *will* actually take place soon.

9. Instruction concerning faithfulness (12:42-48). Peter wanted to know if the parable on watchfulness was to include the disciples (12:41). Jesus replied that it included Peter and anyone who wished to be a wise servant. The greatest quality of a servant is faithfulness, not necessarily ability (1 Cor. 4:1-2).

Faithfulness will be rewarded by the master when He returns (12:42-43). Jesus then gave a warning to those who presumed a delay in the return of the Master. Those with that attitude would develop a false sense of independence and power and would begin to do evil. (A conscious recognition of the any-moment return of Christ is a great deterrent to sin in the life). Though a servant might seem to get away with evil living, the master would eventually return and set things right (12:46-48).

Jesus' statement that the particularly wicked servant was to be assigned a place with the unbelievers (12:46) must be understood in the context of the theocracy. (See also Matt. 24:43-51.) The nation of Israel was in a covenant relationship with God. They were (and are) the only nation with whom God has made a covenant (the church is not a nation but is under the "New Covenant"). Leaders in that nation, such as the priests, were the servants of God and yet could be unbelievers. Jesus probably had these and many of the Pharisees in mind when He spoke this warning. But the application is universal. All will eventually give account to the great Creator God for what they, as His creatures, have done. Those with greater knowledge have greater responsibility and accountability (12:47-48).

10. Instruction concerning the effect of His coming (12:49-53). In reflecting on His own return, Jesus uttered some emotionally packed remarks about His first coming, remarks that reveal something of the tremendous personal anguish He was experiencing (12:49-50). His coming would either burn up (judgment) or purify (life) men and cause division (12:51-53 and Matt. 10:34-36). History has shown this to be true again and again as the truth has brought division within families and groups.

11. Instruction concerning the signs of the times (12:54-59). In continuing the discussion of His comings, the Lord Jesus chastised the crowd for their failure to see all the signs that pointed to Him as Messiah. The miracles and the truth that He so forcefully spoke were clear and obvious evidences from God that Jesus was the long-awaited Messiah. Yet, they had ignored those facts. They had the intelligence to discern the signs in nature, but they had disregarded the greater signs from God. If they did not change, judgment awaited them (12:57-59).

12. Instruction concerning repentance (13:1-9). Jesus' teaching of judgment and punishment (chapter 12) were interrupted by some who pointed to a recent example of men who were evidently punished. Pilate had killed some Galileans while they were in the act of sacrificing animals in the Temple. Undoubtedly the bloodthirsty Pilate was given this opportunity to turn his soldiers loose by some rebellion on the part of these Galileans or by the breaking of some Roman law (the Galileans had openly resisted Rome on numerous occasions). It was a common notion that those who died unusual or violent deaths were exceptionally sinful people who were being judged by God. Jesus denied the validity of this theory and warned His hearers that they must genuinely repent or face a similar fate—that of dying in an unrepentant and lost condition.

Jesus then made reference to another calamity in which eighteen had died in Jerusalem near the pool of Siloam when part of the ancient wall collapsed (13:4). This incident, not recorded anywhere else, was used to deny the unusual sinfulness of these eighteen and again to emphasize the urgent need to repent while there was opportunity to do so. The parable that follows (13:6-9), found only in Luke, stresses the point that opportunity to repent does not last forever. True repentance is evidenced by fruitfulness in one's life. This parable of the barren fig tree was primarily a warning to fruitless Israel. For three years or so the Lord had sought for spiritual fruit and had found none. Fruitless Israel would be judged. What was true of Israel can be applied to individuals today who claim a relationship with God but bear no spiritual fruit in their lives.

13. Instruction concerning Israel's need (13:10-17). The keeping of the Sabbath day was a critical issue in the rejection of Christ by Israel's leaders. Once again Luke records a Sabbath day healing and the resulting controversy. Again the setting was a synagogue. A woman with a long-term physical affliction caused by Satan was instantaneously healed (13:11, 12, 16). The synagogue ruler angrily denounced this miracle as a violation of the Sabbath rest, when no work should be done. Jesus responded to the ruler by explaining that acts of mercy and necessity are not Sabbath day violations (13:15-16). Jesus further denounced the hypocrisy of the ruler (and all those who agreed with his statement) by noting that they engaged in acts of mercy and necessity on the Sabbath when they would rescue and care for their animals. The result of this incident was further humiliation to Jesus' enemies and a greater respect on the part of many people. This is the last time that Luke tells us that Jesus taught in one of their synagogues.

14. Instruction concerning the kingdom program (13:18-21). After the interruption (13:10, 11), Jesus continued to teach. As He often did, He spoke of the kingdom of God. He likened the kingdom to a mustard seed and to leaven (also in Matt. 13:31-33 and Mark 4:30-32). It would have a small, insignificant beginning and yet would quickly grow large. It would also be permeated with evil as time went by. (In order to sense the significance of these kingdom parables they need to be interpreted in the fuller context of Matthew 13. There the mysteries of the kingdom were revealed, and Jesus taught the simultaneous growth of truth and error within the kingdom.)[4]

15. Instruction while traveling toward Jerusalem (13:22-30). Luke again reminds his readers that the days of Jesus' earthly ministry were drawing to a conclusion (13:22) and that Jerusalem was the focus of His ministry. Though this portion took place on another occasion, it is connected with the previous section in subject matter. Someone raised a question regarding the number who would enter the kingdom. Many in Israel believed that because of the covenant God made with

4. J. Dwight Pentecost, *Things to Come* (Grand Rapids: Dunham, 1964), pp. 145-49.

Abraham just about every Israelite would be a participant in the kingdom. However, both John the Baptist and the Lord Jesus made abundantly clear that bloodline and covenant did not guarantee an individual's place in the kingdom. Only faith opened the door of the kingdom (note Matt. 3:5-11 and John 8:33-47). Jesus informed His listeners that it is an eternally fatal thing to reject the King, because one who does cannot enter His kingdom. Here Jesus also implied that many Israelites would not be a part of the kingdom, whereas those of the Gentile nations, from every point on the compass, would be present.

16. Instruction concerning Jerusalem (13:31-35). Jesus was ministering in the region of Perea, which was under Herod Antipas's jurisdiction when some Pharisees warned Jesus that Herod desired to kill Him (as he had killed John the Baptist). It is hard from the text to determine if these Pharisees were genuinely concerned about Jesus' safety or if they had evil motives. In any case, Jesus made it clear that He would continue His ministry without any interruption. Jesus not only declared that He would leave Herod's jurisdiction only when He knew His ministry was completed. He also called Herod "that fox."

> The person described as a fox is looked down upon as weak and wily, and as lacking real power and dignity. Whereas Antipas wanted to be represented as a real threat, his true character and weakness are laid bare by Jesus . . . the cunning schemes of that petty potentate, the fox, were futile before the Great King, the lion.[5]

Even though Jesus was not intimidated by these threats, He nevertheless reaffirmed that His ministry was rapidly coming to a close. The "third day" (13:32-33) carries the idea of a short time or the end of a definite time, or probably both.[6] The

5. Harold Hoehner, *Herod Antipas* (Grand Rapids: Zondervan, 1980), pp. 220-21.
6. Leon Morris, *The Gospel According to St. Luke* (Grand Rapids: Eerdmans, 1982), p. 228.

thought of the end of His ministry and of His coming death caused Jesus to sorrow over the terrible fate that awaited unrepentant Israel, as represented by its chief city, Jerusalem.

17. Instruction in the house of a Pharisee (14:1-24). On a Sabbath day, Jesus was invited to dinner by an important leader of the Pharisees (perhaps he was a member of the Great Sanhedrin). It was obviously not a relaxed, friendly gathering, as Jesus was being watched closely (14:1). Never shrinking from a challenge, He used this occasion to forcefully teach some needed lessons.

First, Jesus healed a man who was sick (14:2-6). Once again He silenced His enemies by making it clear that doing good was not a violation of the principle of the Sabbath and they themselves did good things on the Sabbath (14:5). Their inconsistency was again made so obvious that they had no rebuttal to make.

Next, Jesus gave a parable (perhaps thinking of Prov. 25:6-7) as He observed the other invited guests jostling with one another to get to the places of greatest honor (14:7-11). Jesus warned them of the possible embarrassment that could be theirs if the host asked them to give up their places to persons considered to be more worthy. But more important than that was the spiritual truth that true exaltation comes to one who is truly humble. These religious men were proud, and God is said to resist the proud (James 4:6). The truly humble person sees himself as God sees him, and that eliminates pride and arrogance from his life. God honors such a person (Luke 1:48, 51-52).

Jesus continued by directing His next words to the host of the dinner (14:12-14). They were radical words then, and they are now also. He stated that one needs to go beyond mutual hospitality. Be generous toward those who cannot repay, Jesus said. Using one's resources in such a manner will bring reward (Luke 16:1-13; 1 Tim. 6:17-19).

One final lesson from that eventful dinner was recorded by Luke (14:15-24). One of the guests uttered a pious beatitude concerning the joy of being in God's kingdom (obviously including himself in that number). Jesus seized that opportunity to forcefully declare that not all who are invited to the feast of God (the kingdom) would enter in and partake. It was common when giving a formal dinner to issue two invitations, one inviting the guests and a second announcing that the feast was made ready. In this parable, many were invited, but, when informed that the feast was ready, all gave lame excuses for not attending. The rebuffed host then invited the many outcasts of the city and surrounding areas to come and fill his banquet hall. The invited guests were not allowed to come and eat. This was yet another warning to the nation of Israel that their place in the feast (the kingdom) was dependent on their response to God's invitation. They must believe and receive their King if they would be part of the kingdom. The rejection by Israel is anticipated as is the inclusion of the Gentiles (the many outcasts).

18. Instruction concerning discipleship (14:25-35). At this late date in His ministry Jesus was still attracting great crowds. But large numbers never seemed to impress the Lord Jesus, as He was looking for those few people of quality and commitment to come and follow Him. On this occasion He once again addressed the issue of being a disciple (see the discussion on Luke 9:23). Three times in His message Jesus stated that a person could not be His disciple if certain requirements were not met (14:26-27, 33). These requirements for discipleship, not salvation, again included the willingness to openly identify with Christ and also the placing of Christ as the supreme master of one's life. In this passage, the Lord Jesus emphasized yet another requirement. He demanded that those who would follow Him consider carefully the personal cost of discipleship.

Using two illustrations, one of a man building a tower (14:28-30) and the other of a king going to war (14:31-32), the Lord communicated the single truth that significant decisions in life require forethought and evaluation. No wise man enters into an important project or relationship without giving the matter serious thought so that a rational decision can be made. To be a genuine follower of Christ requires serious and realistic thought regarding the cost and consequences of such a choice. Jesus stated that a person must say good-bye to everything that is important to him (14:33). Practically speaking, the idea is that any believer who seriously desires to be Christ's servant must consciously, specifically, prayerfully say good-bye to all people, goals, desires, and possessions that are important to him. Christ must have no rivals in his life. That does not mean that these things will be taken away from the believer. But should the sovereign, loving Lord remove them from his life (knowing what is best for His servant), the believer will have already said farewell to them.

Jesus concluded this discussion on discipleship by noting the consequences of not following Him (14:34-35). Discipleship was (and is) a voluntary matter. There are, rather obviously, some consequences to one's choice on the issue. Jesus stated that the one who chooses not to give the leadership of his life to Christ will have a life that resembles salt that has lost its saltiness. Salt that has lost its seasoning has no value and has lost its purpose for existence. And so, the believer who chooses not to fulfill these requirements and follow Christ as a disciple will have a life with little value and purpose.

19. Instruction concerning God's attitude toward sinners (15:1-32). One of several things about Jesus that bothered the Pharisees was the regular contact that He had with the rejects of Jewish society. Publicans were Jewish tax collectors for the Roman government and were considered traitors. "Sinner" was a designation for one who was either immoral, irreligious, or a nonpracticing Jew. These "sinners" listened to and ate with Jesus (15:2).

> Table fellowship anywhere in the world is a relatively serious matter. This is especially true in the Middle East. . . . The meal is a special sign of acceptance. . . . Jesus is set forth in the text as engaging in some such

> social relationship with publicans and sinners. Small wonder the Pharisees were upset. In addition to "eating with sinners" there is the possibility that Jesus was himself hosting sinners.[7]

The Pharisees objected to such a close association with sinners by one who claimed to be from God, since they believed such individuals were unclean and to be avoided. They believed that God was not pleased with these people and that He delighted in their death.

The Lord Jesus told three stories that were similar in structure to reveal the true attitude of God toward the lost (in obvious contrast to the attitude of the Pharisees). In these three parables, Jesus taught that God values that which is lost and that there is great joy over finding the lost.

The first story, the lost sheep (15:3-7), and the second story, the lost coin (15:8-10), both underscore that we do value those things that are lost. In fact, when something is lost we become even more conscious of its importance and value and when it is found there is relief and joy. Jesus instructed the Pharisees that God is that way regarding people who are lost (15:7, 10). God has a seeking love. Yet, these religious leaders of Israel who were designated as shepherds (as in Ezek. 34 and Zech. 11) evidenced little interest in lost sheep.

The third story, the lost son (15:11-32), is much longer and far more detailed. Jesus set the stage by telling His hearers that a man had two sons. The focus of the story is initially on the younger son (the prodigal) and then shifts to the older brother later on in the story (15:12, 25).

The Lord began the story with the younger son's making an unbelievable request, that of asking for his inheritance before his father's death (15:12). Such a thing was unheard of in that day, since it was essentially wishing for the father's death and would, therefore, have been a terrible insult to the father.

7. Kenneth E. Bailey, *Poet and Peasant and Through Peasant Eyes* (Grand Rapids: Eerdmans, 1980), pp. 142-43.

> The prodigal's actions are all the more remarkable because his request is twofold. He requests the division of the inheritance. His request is granted. But this gives him ownership without the right to dispose of his share. The property is his but he cannot sell it. He wants more, so he pressures his father into granting him full disposition immediately. . . . Here the younger son gets, and thus is assumed to have demanded, disposition to which, even more explicitly, he had no right until the death of his father. The implication of "Father, I cannot wait for you to die" underlies both requests. It is even stronger in the second.[8]

The insulted, rejected father responded with unbelievable grace and kindness to this insolent, rebellious son and gave him his request. The son then left his father's house and journeyed far away. In a distant country he squandered his inheritance. Family property lost to Gentiles was considered a serious offense.

Soon after the prodigal's money ran out a severe famine struck the area (15:14) with the result that he ended up living and eating with pigs (15:13-16). He evidently was reduced to the point where he was eating the wild carob of the Middle East, which was a thorny shrub with bitter berries having little nutritional value.

Coming to his senses, the younger son decided to return home, confess his failures, and offer himself as a hired servant in his father's house (15:17-19). In the category of a hired servant he would have no rights of sonship. He probably realized that when he came back he would have to face the hostility of the family and the community for his offensive actions. This would be an evidence of the true nature of his repentance.

When the young man returned, the father spotted him a long way off (no doubt because he was looking for him), ran to him, and repeatedly kissed him (15:20). In that culture it was con-

8. Ibid., p. 164.

sidered undignified and somewhat humiliating for an older man to run in public. But love and compassion drove the father to hurry to embrace his wayward son. The kiss given by the father was

> a sign of reconciliation and forgiveness. When a serious quarrel has taken place in the village and reconciliation is achieved, a part of the ceremony enacted as a sacrament of reconciliation is a public kiss by leading men involved.[9]

The prodigal son fully repented and was given the best robe (a sign of acceptance), a gold ring (signifying authority and trust), and sandals (a sign of a free man). All of these items beautifully picture our restoration to the heavenly Father when a man receives Christ's great gift of salvation. The killing of the fatted calf was for special occasions only. The joy of the father was great.

The focus of the Lord's parable shifts at this point to the older son, who most likely represented the Pharisees (15:25-32). The older son, like the Pharisee, labored diligently in the father's field but was not in sympathy with the father. In the story, the elder brother did not attempt to reconcile the prodigal and his father; he did not go into the far country seeking his wayward brother; and he certainly did not rejoice at the brother's return and the father's acceptance of him. The elder brother's self-righteous attitude as well as his failure to understand what it meant to be a son (he had the spirit of a slave and not a son) and what it meant to be a father was seen in his conversation with his father (15:29-30).

It should also be observed that the older brother's refusal to be a part of the celebration would have constituted a grave insult to his father, and his public argument with his father would have been humiliating and offensive. The break in relationship between the older son and the father was nearly as

9. Ibid., p. 182.

severe as the one between the younger son and the father. The elder son was just as lost as the younger. The younger son was alienated from his father while away from the house. The elder son was alienated from his father while in the house. It is instructive to note that the father was equally concerned with this son and sought him out and expressed his love for him. God loves the unrighteous *and* the self-righteous.

20. Instruction concerning wealth (16:1-31). Jesus, without pausing, continued His teaching to the tax gatherers, sinners, Pharisees, and the disciples (15:1-2; 16:1, 14). There are two main teachings in this chapter separated by a rebuke to the Pharisees. The first teaching is the parable of the unrighteous steward (16:1-13).

Once again the Lord Jesus used a setting that was quite familiar to His hearers. In this parable the subject is a man who was a steward. The role of a steward was one of great responsibility and trust. It was fairly common in Palestine in that day for there to be absentee landlords, who entrusted their lands to stewards. The steward would be over the tenant farmers and would receive from the tenant farmers an agreed-upon percentage of their crops as rent. (Old Testament illustrations of stewards are Eliezer in Gen. 24 and Joseph in Gen. 39). This steward, however, was unfaithful and was caught stealing from his master. The master, upon receiving word of the situation, expressed shock at this betrayal. The "you" is emphasized (16:2) and might read, "You, of all people, have betrayed my trust!" An audit was demanded, and the steward realized that he shortly would have no job.

He had not lost his job yet, but it was just a matter of time ("my master *is taking* the stewardship away from me"). He was embarrassed to beg, and physical labor was out of the question (16:3). He came up with a plan. Since his signature was still good, he called in the tenant farmers and reduced the bill of each one. The result would be that these farmers would be favorable toward him. Also, he involved them in his own crime and now, if necessary, could exercise some gentle blackmail.

The key to this parable is the master's statement (16:8*a*). The master praised the steward not for his theft but for his foresight. The steward had used his present opportunity to provide for the future. This is the right use of money. The wise steward (the believer) is to use his present opportunities to invest in eternity.

Jesus then explained that generally unbelievers are far more shrewd in money matters than are believers (16:8*b*). Furthermore, He said, His followers should influence others (in spiritual and eternal matters) with their money and material possessions (16:9). "Mammon" is money and the things that money can buy. It is probably called "unrighteous" mammon because of the manner in which it is generally used. Believers are to use their material possessions as tools for God to influence people for Christ. Money (mammon) will one day fail. But those influenced for Christ will be waiting in heaven to receive the "investor." Such use of money will have eternal dividends. The apostle Paul makes the same point in 1 Timothy 6:17-19.

Jesus continued to explain and apply truth regarding money (16:10). He pointed out that money is really not nearly as significant as spiritual matters. But if a man is not faithful in the use of the lesser things (money), then God will not commit to him greater things (spiritual matters). A slave could be the servant of only one. Jesus declared that serving money removes one from the role as a servant of God (16:13).

The Pharisees responded negatively to the parable (16:14). Generally the Pharisees were wealthy, and they assumed that "whom the Lord loveth, He maketh wealthy." They were sure that God had blessed them because they had been faithful in keeping the law. When a very poor rabbi (Jesus) spoke against wealth, they thought that he must be less than righteous, one who did not faithfully keep the law (such as violating the Sabbath). He became the subject of their derision. But Jesus rebuked them, informing them that God was not impressed with their outward displays of generosity and righteousness (16:15). He further explained that they could not force their way into the kingdom with their own righteousness (16:16).

The coming of John the Baptist had brought a progress in the revelation of God. The gospel of the kingdom was a new dimension, which emphasized in a greater way heart attitudes and not simply external righteousness. Jesus then stated that the law would not be abandoned, however, until every part is fulfilled (16:17). The next statement (16:18) seems to be an illustration that the moral principles of the law are still in effect.

The second major teaching in this chapter is the parable of the rich man and Lazarus (16:19-31). Several controversial matters are related to this account. First, what is the subject? In the context of the chapter, the subject is money and its use. This story is an illustration of the wrong use of money and the wrong attitudes toward money. The rich man used his money selfishly, revealing his true spiritual condition. Lazarus, the beggar, was the one who actually possessed the true riches. The scoffing Pharisees (16:14) were being told that it was not true that "whom the Lord loveth, He maketh wealthy." This parable is not primarily a discussion of the afterlife, and one must therefore be careful in using it out of its context.

A second issue relating to this account is the problem of whether or not this is a parable or an actual historical account. First, it has been pointed out that Jesus' use of the name *Lazarus* suggests that it was an actual event and not a parable. But Lazarus means "God has helped" and is a perfect name for this story to describe the situation. Man had not helped this poor man, but God had. Furthermore, Lazarus was a common name and so would be relatively meaningless if the Lord was trying to identify a certain situation. Why did not the Lord give the rich man's name if He was identifying a specific situation? Second, it has been noted that this story is not called a parable (as Jesus did in 15:3 and other places). But it is clear that not all Jesus' parables were called such by Him as He began to tell the story (the first one here in chapter 16 is not called a parable either). Third, to make this an actual incident raises some theological problems. For example, how can Abraham appear in bodily form before the resurrection? How can there be communication between the saved and the lost? Fourth, to see this as a parable does not in any way negate the horrors and agony of hell. Some who wish to make this an actual incident have believed that to do otherwise lessens the reality of hell. But there is much in Scripture that verifies the terrible future that awaits the man without Christ as his Savior. It is best to take this teaching as a parable.

Jesus began the parable by introducing His listeners (which included the wealthy Pharisees) to two men. The first man was quite rich. He dressed in the finest of clothes and each day enjoyed his wealth to the fullest. He used his money for personal pleasure and recognition. The second man was a poor, sick beggar who was laid (or "was cast") at the gate of this rich man in hopes of getting scraps from his table. As he lay there hungry and sick, dogs came and licked his sores.

> . . . it is not to be understood as an alleviation, but as an aggravation of his ills, that he was left to the dogs, which in Scripture are always represented as unclean animals.[10]

Jesus then said that both of these men died, with Lazarus going to Paradise ("Abraham's bosom") and the rich man ending up in hades (16:22-23). In conscious agony the rich man made two requests, neither of which was granted (16:24, 27). First, he requested that Lazarus be sent to him with some water to cool him and relieve some of his suffering. This request made to Abraham may suggest that some pride was still resident in him as he still saw Lazarus as one who should serve him. At any rate, the request was denied, and it was noted that the separation between them was permanent. The second request was that his family be warned. The rich man suggested Lazarus be returned to life on earth and give a warning to the rich man's brothers. This too was rejected. Abraham noted that the rich man's brothers had all the information that they needed in the Word of God. If they would not listen to the voice of God

10. Alfred Edersheim, *The Life and Times of Jesus the Messiah,* 2 vols. (New York: Longmans, Green, 1900), 2:279.

through Moses and the prophets, then they would not listen to God's voice through Lazarus. The miraculous return to earth of Lazarus would not bring about faith (16:31).

In this parable, the Lord Jesus forcefully told the Pharisees that wealth was no sign of God's favor, nor was it to be viewed as a reward for righteous behavior. Conversely, poverty was not to be seen as evidence of God's disfavor.

Although this parable's major emphasis was on money, it also teaches some facts about the afterlife. Some of the details might be debated, but the story does teach that there is conscious life immediately after death, that the saved and the lost are eternally separated, and that the lost carry with them some memories of their earthly experiences. It is another awesome reminder that men who foolishly ignore the life that God offers will spend eternity away from Him.

21. Instruction concerning forgiveness (17:1-6). The Lord Jesus (probably on another occasion) talked to His disciples, warning them about being stumbling stones to those around them, especially to children. He said that is was better to die a violent death than to lead others into sin (17:2). The Lord then looked at the other side of the issue of offenses. When a person offends you, Jesus said, rebuke him to his face (not behind his back). If the guilty one shows signs of repentance he is to be forgiven. (Note that other passages develop this subject of forgiveness and should be included in the study—Matt. 18:21-35; Eph. 4:30-32; Col. 3:13). Jesus explained that there should be no limits to forgiveness, especially toward one who is genuinely repentant. The disciples were impressed deeply by what the Lord had said (17:5), and they requested the faith and strength necessary to live according to this high standard of conduct. The Lord emphasized (17:6) the kind of faith that is needed. It is not the amount of faith that is determinative, but the object of one's faith. Faith must be in the Lord Himself.

22. Instruction concerning service (17:7-10). The following teaching by the Lord Jesus was built upon the common Middle

553.82
5.82
559 64
56.10
503.54
95
408 54
160
248 54
120
128 54
24.26
104 28
535
639 28
434
205 28
2
406.29
163 50
241 78

10 11

10 11

Doron Segal
$307.00

302 762 3232
Bill Marton

Eastern understanding of the relationship between masters and slaves. It is an important teaching because it helps give balance in our understanding of the relationship that exists between Christ and believers. As believers we know that Jesus is our friend, brother, and fellow-heir. But He is also our master, and this bit of instruction is valuable as a corrective to certain false views and attitudes that some Christians have.

In the story, Jesus spoke of a slave (bondslave) who had worked diligently during the day and returned to his master's house. Upon arriving the master would require that he now prepare the meal. After the master had eaten, then the slave would be permitted to eat and rest. Jesus also noted that the master would not thank the slave for doing what he was supposed to do (17:9). In our day such a situation at first seems harsh. But it must be remembered that the slave had (in that culture) a deep sense of security, worth, and meaning to his life by being associated with and servant to a rich man.

The story communicates two great truths. First, the master had absolute authority over the servant. The master's will was to become the slave's will. Second, the servant's only proper attitude is one of humility and submission. When Jesus stated that the master would not thank the servant for his work (17:9), He did not mean that the master might not say, "Thank you," or, "nice work," to his sevant. He means that the master is not indebted to the servant for the work that he did. Jesus was telling His disciples that no matter how much we obey God, He never becomes indebted to us or is obligated to fulfill our desires. Our only proper attitude is to view ourselves as not deserving of any reward. We are servants to whom nothing is owed (17:10). There is the tendency on the part of believers who labor diligently for the Lord to sometimes think they should have life a little easier or a little better—that God owes them something.

23. Instruction concerning thankfulness (17:11-19). Luke once again reminds his readers that Jesus' goal is Jerusalem (17:11). As Jesus came near to a certain unnamed village, ten leprous men called Him by name, requesting to be cleansed. They called to Him from a distance, obeying the Mosaic law concerning lepers. Jesus evidently did not approach them but simply commanded them to go and show themselves to the priest. As they went in obedience to Christ's command, they were completely cleansed of their leprosy. However, only one of the ten, when the cleansing took place, turned back to give thanks to the one who healed him. He is the only one who is said to have given thanks to God also. And the thankful man was a Samaritan. The Lord Jesus was evidently disappointed with the thankless attitude of the others. Offering praise and thanksgiving is not only the right thing to do, it is one of those things that pleases God and brings glory to Him (1 Thess. 5:18; Heb. 13:15-16). In the account, not only was the Samaritan cleansed from his leprosy, but he also received spiritual cleansing (17:19).

24. Instruction concerning the second coming (17:20—18:8). In response to the Pharisees' question about when the kingdom would arrive, the Lord gave instruction about the end times. First, He pointed out to the Pharisees (who were probably looking for some sort of political messiah to rescue them from Rome) that the kingdom was "in your midst" (17:21). A spiritual kingdom was not in the unbelieving Pharisees. The phrase is best taken to mean that the kingdom was "among them" in the person of the King. He was in their midst, and yet they did not acknowledge Him as the Messiah.

The followers of Christ would long for His coming, especially when things got difficult (17:22-24). They, in this frame of mind, could be deceived by false claims that Jesus had returned. They were encouraged not to listen to such reports, because when Jesus returns it will be obvious to all.

Jesus did let them know that there would be delay in the coming of the kingdom, as it was essential that He would be rejected and killed by that generation of Israel. Later on Jesus would give a more detailed discussion of the delay of the kingdom (19:11-27).

Next Jesus talked about some of the conditions that would exist on the earth before the kingdom was established (17:26-31). The conditions of the world before Christ returns at His second coming would be quite similar to the conditions of the world in the time of Noah (17:26) and the condition of Sodom in the days of Lot (17:29). See Genesis 6:1-11; 19:1-8. There seems to be a twofold emphasis here: (1) an utter abandonment to worldliness with no real concern for God and (2) a total immersion into evil of all kinds. These would be general indicators, but as they grow in intensity the believer is to be alert.

After giving some information about the future, the Lord Jesus issued warnings (17:32-37). Lot's wife was destroyed along with the citizens of Sodom even though she had left the city. In her heart she longed for wicked Sodom and turned back. She did not take seriously the judgments of God and perished as a result. Those who will willingly stand for Christ in the Tribulation period will probably be martyred, but in a sense will gain (17:33). On the other hand, one who goes along with the system of wickedness in that day (thus demonstrating that he is an unbeliever) will eventually lose his life. He then spoke of those who would be taken and those who would be left. This is not a discussion of the rapture. Those who are left at the end of the tribulation period are left to enter Messiah's kingdom, those who are taken are taken away in judgment. The Lord Jesus spoke of this judgment of the living at the end of the Tribulation period in the parable of the sheep and the goats and the parable of the ten virgins (Matt. 25). In the final statement (17:37) about the vultures gathering over the dead body, Jesus informed them very generally when these events would take place. This saying seems to be a way of stating that where the spiritually dead are located, there will be judgment.

The final words in His discussion of the second coming were a parable on prayer. The setting for this parable is the Tribulation period (18:7-8). During that time things will not go well for God's people. They will pray for the righteous judgment of God. So successful will the oppressors of God's people be that the characteristic of the people on the earth will be unbelief (Rev. 12:12; 13:7; 17:6). The parable itself was about a widow who persistently brought her case before a judge who was uncaring about her or her problem. He would not have acted on her behalf if it had not been for the fact that she would not let him alone. In order to get rid of her, he acted on her case. Jesus taught His followers, whether in the Tribulation period or today, to be persistent in praying. We really have only two options available (18:1). We can keep praying or give up. The second option has no future in it for us. (See the discussion on Luke 11:1-13.)

25. Instruction concerning self-righteousness (18:9-14). The parable of the Pharisee and the tax collector is not really a parable on prayer. It is a parable on the subject of righteousness and how one obtains righteousness. In the parable, the Pharisee and the tax collector both go up to the Temple, presumably at the time of public worship. Other people were evidently present, since the Pharisee was said to pray by himself and the tax collector (18:13) was some distance away (from the other worshipers). Perhaps this praying was going on during the time of the incense offering (Luke 1:10), which was the time for private praying during the public worship time.

The Pharisee stood apart from others because he considered himself spiritually superior to all the rest. In his prayer, everything he said was undoubtedly true (18:11-12). He did tithe, fast, and avoid the uncleanesses that were mentioned. But when he left the Temple that day and went home, he was not one whom God had justified (18:14). He thought that the things that exalted him in his own eyes and in the eyes of others also gave him merit before God. This was a clear case of self-righteousness, which will never bring a man into a right standing before God (Rom. 10:1-4; Gal. 2:16).

The tax collector (publican) was just what he said he was—a sinner. He was undoubtedly known for his cheating and a wide assortment of vices. But he recognized the fact that he stood guilty before God and prayed accordingly (18:13). (Remember that the tax collector could have prayed and thanked God that he was not like the hypocritical Pharisee!) His cry was based on sacrifice. He prayed that God would be propitious (satisfied). His prayer for cleansing was answered, and he left the Temple and went home that day a justified man (18:14). The great truth of the New Testament is that God is satisfied with the death of Jesus Christ and can therefore cleanse anyone who comes to Him (1 John 2:1-2).

26. Instruction concerning entrance into the kingdom (18:15-30). The Jews were very impressed with the teachings of the Lord as well as the miracles that He performed. And while they were often unclear about His person (John the Baptist? Elijah? Jeremiah?), they perceived He must be from God. Therefore, many parents brought their little ones to Jesus for His blessing. One day as some were bringing them, the disciples thwarted their intentions, probably informing these parents that Jesus was much too busy to tend to such insignificant matters. Jesus kindly rebuked His disciples, informing them that children are very important (18:16-17). Jesus said that in order for a person (adult or child) to enter the kingdom there must be childlike faith. To be saved there must be complete trust in God (and the things that God has said). This passage is inconclusive on the subject of the salvation of infants who die in infancy. It would certainly be supportive of the idea that children who die are a part of the kingdom of God.

The issue of salvation and one's place in the kingdom continued with the discussion with the rich young ruler. As Jesus was ready to leave that area (Mark 10:17) a young man approached Him with a question about eternal life. This man, a ruler of some sort, addressed Jesus as "good." Jesus reminded him that only God is good—goodness was seen by the Jews as an attribute of God alone. Jesus was not denying that He was good but was only trying to get the man to reflect on his own words. The ruler evidently did not see the significance of what Jesus said. The ruler wanted to know what it was that he had *to do* in order to gain eternal life. He evidently was not there or was not listening when Jesus explained that it was childlike faith that brought one into the kingdom. But since he posed his question around doing something, the Lord responded in like manner.

He claimed to have kept all of the commandments (18:21). Jesus, knowing that the man was only deceiving himself, told him to do one more thing and that was to sell all he owned, give it to the poor, and come follow Jesus (18:22). His inability to do this (because he was so wealthy) revealed that he in fact had not kept the commandments. He loved his money more than he loved his God. He trusted in his money more than he trusted in his God. He left, presumably unsaved.

Jesus used this occasion to once again point out the danger of riches (18:24-25). Riches have the ability to keep a man's affections on material things and off God. Just as it is impossible for a camel to go through the eye of a needle (it is best to interpret this literally), so it is equally impossible for a man in his own strength to overcome the temptation of earthly wealth and be saved. The rich young ruler found Jesus' demands too difficult, and the bystanders found Jesus' statement too difficult (18:26). Still influenced with the mentality that wealth was a sign of the favor of God on a man's life, they assumed that the wealthy had an inside track into the kingdom. If Jesus was right that the rich could not be saved, then what about poor people? Jesus made abundantly clear that salvation is a miraculous work of God. The power of God is able to save men of every condition.

At this point Peter reminded the Lord that he and the others had left their possessions for Him (18:28-30). Jesus responded and said that anyone who really has given up things for *His sake* has the assurance of being part of His kingdom. Such acts are motivated by a heart that has been changed.

27. Instruction concerning His death (18:31-34). The next words of instruction were for the disciples' ears only, so Jesus took the twelve aside. Once again He spoke to them of His death. In fact, this is the fourth time that Luke has recorded such teaching about His death. But now it was even more significant since the day of His crucifixion was coming soon (in the next chapter we find ourselves in the last week of the Lord's life). His disciples were informed that His death was not a change in God's program, but rather this was something spoken of by the prophets of old. Death will be unable to hold Him, however, and He will rise again. Some of the details surrounding His suffering were known by the Lord and were related to the disciples. Jesus knew that He would be spit upon, physically abused, scourged, and then killed. Luke notes that the Gentiles would have a part in His suffering, whereas Matthew observes that the Jewish leaders would play a role as well. Luke states that Jesus would be killed by these wicked men, whereas Matthew gives the detail that it was death by crucifixion (Matt. 20:19). The disciples evidently were still clinging to their hope of an immediate establishment of Messiah's kingdom, since Judas Iscariot was still there. And they, at that point in time, simply could not put together the idea of a ruling and dying Messiah.

Perhaps one of the great truths from this portion is the love and courage of the Lord Jesus. It is one thing to have tragedy strike unexpectedly and endure the agony of the event. It is quite another thing to know months in advance the terrible details of suffering that awaits you and voluntarily face them. Such it was with the Lord Jesus.

28. Ministry to the blind man at Jericho (18:35-43). The Lord Jesus was clearly headed for Jerusalem and His time of suffering. Luke traces His journey with several geographic notations (see fig. 3.2).

After crossing the Jordan river, the Lord Jesus came to Jericho, and it was there that He encountered a blind beggar by the name of Bartimaeus (Mark 10:46 gives his name). There was a very large crowd with Jesus, and as this multitude approached the city, the blind man (who was evidently in the city itself) heard the commotion. When he came to understand that Jesus was coming, he evidently immediately and persistently

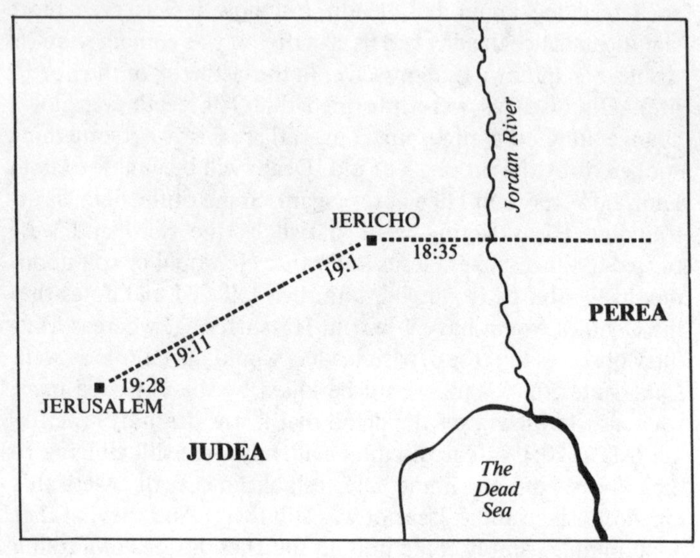

Fig. 3.2

began calling out to Jesus and addressing Him as the "Son of David" (a messianic term). By identifying Jesus as the Messiah, the blind man was claiming a messianic blessing of healing. Undoubtedly the blind man knew Isaiah 35:5, which promised that when the Messiah would come, blind men would be able to see. He believed that Jesus of Nazareth was the Messiah. How long he called out before Jesus finally heard him is not known. But he was persistent in spite of being told to be quiet. Jesus approached him and allowed him to make his request (18:41). The blind man did not hesitate in unbelief but immediately made his request. Jesus responded to Bartimaeus's faith in Him and healed him. And Bartimaeus becomes a worthy example to us of faith that is persistent and unshaken by the discouraging comments of men. Faith in the Son of David always brings mercy and blessing.

29. Ministry to Zacchaeus (19:1-10). Again in the vicinity of Jericho, the Lord Jesus encountered a man who was a rich tax collector. The man's name was Zacchaeus, and he was a "chief" tax collector, probably signifying that he was the head of that particular district and that others under him collected the taxes. Zacchaeus had heard about Jesus and desired to see him. But when the multitudes came by he was unable to see Jesus because he was short of stature and no doubt nobody wished to let this unpopular tax collector through. So he climbed a tree to watch Jesus pass by. But Jesus did not pass by; instead He stopped and addressed Zacchaeus. Jesus informed Zacchaeus that He would be staying with him. Undoubtedly Jesus understood this to be a part of His ministry. Zacchaeus gladly received Jesus, but the crowds disapproved of this fellowship with a tax collector (19:7).

Jesus stopped on this occasion because He knew that salvation would come to this man. Zacchaeus's repentance was seen by external acts (as true repentance always is identified). He volunteered to give half of his money to the poor, and he promised to restore fourfold anything that was taken fraudulently (which was far greater than the law demanded for voluntary restitution, Lev. 6:5). Zacchaeus now became a true, spiritual son of Abraham (19:9) and an example of why the Lord Jesus came—"to seek and to save that which was lost" (19:10).

30. Instruction concerning the delayed kingdom (19:11-27). The next incident took place in or near the house of Zacchaeus. The Lord Jesus was about seventeen miles away from Jerusalem, and many were still anticipating the immediate setting up of the kingdom (19:11). This parable of the nobleman and the pounds (minas) was given to again inform the disciples and others that the establishment of the kingdom would be delayed because of the unbelief and rejection of that generation in Israel.

The nobleman represents Christ, and the far country is to be interpreted as heaven. Jesus is going to go to heaven and receive the royal authority for the kingdom. (Note that the kingdom is the place where He was at the moment He was speaking.) He will set up that kingdom at His glorious second coming.

> The imagery of the parable was undoubtedly drawn from actual events in the political history of the times. It was a regular procedure for native princes to journey to Rome to receive their right to rule. For this purpose, during our Lord's youth at Nazareth, the son of Herod the Great, Archelaus, went to Rome. He was so hated of the Jews that they sent a delegation after him to protest against his enthronement, but to no avail. And upon his return Archelaus rewarded his supporters with certain cities and took vengeance on his enemies. Josephus says that his great palace was built at Jericho, perhaps not far from the home of Zacchaeus where the parable was first spoken.[11]

Two groups of individuals are found in the parable (19:13-14). The first group that Christ spoke about were His servants. They were given certain responsibilities and were to "carry on business" while the nobleman was absent (while He was away, prior to the establishment of the kingdom). The second group were the citizens of His territory (the world). The citizens hated Him, and they did not want Him to rule over them (see John 19:15).

Upon his return the nobleman rewarded his faithful servants (the one unfaithful servant lost his reward, 19:24). There were differences in the rewards based upon the diligence of the servants. The citizens, however, were killed, being judged for their refusal to accept him as their ruler.

As the Lord Jesus headed up to Jerusalem it was clear that He had no delusions that He would be accepted with open arms and that the messianic kingdom would be established. He had stated clearly that the setting up of this aspect of the kingdom of God would be postponed. The kingdom would come, but unbelief prohibited it from being a present reality.

11. McClain, *The Greatness of the Kingdom*, p. 341.

4

THE SUFFERING AND SACRIFICE OF JESUS THE SON OF MAN

(LUKE 19:28—23:56)

A. HIS TRIUMPHANT ENTRY (19:28-44)

Jesus arrived at the village of Bethany, which was located about two miles east of Jerusalem. There were deep, but mixed, feelings about Him. The leaders wanted Him dead and had an "all points bulletin" out on Him (see John 11:57). Many loved Him, such as Mary, Martha, and Lazarus. But whatever feelings about Him existed, Jesus knew that it was necessary for Him to fulfill the Old Testament prophecies (such as Zech. 9:9) and present Himself publicly to Israel. This public presentation, which is commonly called the "triumphal entry" was not an event designed to discover whether or not Israel would receive Him. They had already rejected Him. The purpose of this event was to fulfill prophecy.

Specific preparations were made (19:29-34). Two disciples were sent to get a donkey on which no one had ever ridden (in the Old Testament something unused was suitable for sacred purposes). It is possible that the Lord Jesus had made arrangements at an earlier time for the use of the donkey. The disciples returned with the donkey, and the procession to Jerusalem took place (19:35-44). A large number of people participated in or simply observed this procession.

> According to John, the crowds who assembled came from three sources. In 12:12 a pilgrim throng approached Jerusalem from more distant areas. Probably most of

> them came from Galilee where they had witnessed a large part of Jesus' ministry. In 12:17 the crowd that had been in Bethany when Lazarus was raised bore witness (cf. John 11:42). In 12:18 a large Jerusalem crowd flocked out of the city to see the one who had raised Lazarus.[1]

There was much excitement and rejoicing (19:37-38), but some objected to the procession, understanding its messianic implications (19:39). Jesus informed these Pharisees that such praise was right and essential (19:40)

It is not correct to assume that the people understood this event and believed that Jesus was the Messiah. The disciples themselves did not really understand what this procession was all about (see John 12:16). And later in Jerusalem, the crowd simply said, "This is the prophet Jesus from Nazareth" (Matt. 21:11). They did not say, "This is the Messiah," or, "This is the Son of the living God." Only Jesus understood what was happening. As He saw the true situation, spiritual reality overwhelmed Jesus, and He wept ("sobbed audibly"). Israel had not understood, and they had rejected Him. The result was that Jerusalem would be besieged and destroyed (19:43-44). Perhaps the saddest words Jesus uttered were, "You did not recognize the time of your visitation" (19:44). Thousands of people who witnessed the "triumphal entry" are in hell this very hour, because they missed the day of opportunity. This entry into Jerusalem was not really triumphal after all. And sadly, many people today are missing the "day of visitation" in their own, individual lives.

B. HIS CLEANSING OF THE TEMPLE (19:45-48)

The "triumphal entry" took place on a Sunday, and on the following day Jesus cleansed the Temple. Mark 11:11 tells us that Jesus entered the Temple on the day of the "triumphal entry" but did nothing but observe the situation there. However, He returned the next day to cleanse it.

1. Robert L. Thomas and Stanley N. Gundry, *A Harmony of the Gospels* (Chicago: Moody, 1978), p. 176.

THE FINAL WEEK

EVENT	DAY	LUKE*	OTHER GOSPELS
JESUS' TRIUMPHAL ENTRY INTO JERUSALEM	SUNDAY	19:29	MATTHEW, MARK, JOHN
CURSING OF THE FIG TREE	MONDAY	____	MATTHEW, MARK
CLEANSING THE TEMPLE	MONDAY	19:45	MATTHEW, MARK
DISPUTES WITH THE RELIGIOUS LEADERS	TUESDAY	20:1	MATTHEW, MARK
MARY ANOINTS JESUS	TUESDAY	____	MATTHEW, MARK, JOHN
JUDAS BETRAYS JESUS	TUESDAY	22:3	MATTHEW, MARK
JESUS EATS THE LAST SUPPER WITH DISCIPLES	THURSDAY	22:7	MATTHEW, MARK, JOHN
JESUS GIVES THE UPPER ROOM DISCOURSE	THURSDAY	____	JOHN
JESUS IN THE GARDEN OF GETHSEMANE	THURS/FRI	22:39	MATTHEW, MARK, JOHN
JESUS IS ARRESTED IN THE GARDEN	FRIDAY	22:47	MATTHEW, MARK, JOHN
THE TRIALS OF JESUS	FRIDAY	22:52ff.	MATTHEW, MARK, JOHN
—before Annas	"	____	JOHN
—before Caiaphas	"	22:54, 63	MATTHEW, MARK, JOHN
—before the Council	"	22:66	MATTHEW, MARK
—before Pilate	"	23:1	MATTHEW, MARK, JOHN
—before Herod	"	23:6	____
—before Pilate	"	23:13	MATTHEW, MARK, JOHN
THE CRUCIFIXION	FRIDAY	23:26	MATTHEW, MARK, JOHN
SAYING FROM THE CROSS	FRIDAY	23:34	MATTHEW, MARK, JOHN
—Father, forgive. . .	"	23:34	____
—Today shalt thou be. . .	"	23:43	____
—Woman, behold thy. . .	"	____	JOHN
—My God, My God. . .	"	____	MATTHEW, MARK
—I thirst	"	____	JOHN
—It is finished	"	____	JOHN
—Father, into Thy hands I commend. . .	"	23:46	____
JESUS IS BURIED	FRIDAY	23:50	MATTHEW, MARK, JOHN

Fig. 4.1

This was the second time in the Lord's ministry that He forcibly removed the illegal practices (John 2 records the first time He did this). Jesus saw buying and selling in the Temple as a violation of Isaiah 56:7. The leaders, who wanted to kill Him, were powerless against Him as long as there was a great crowd of the common people there, for they greatly admired Him as a man of God.

C. HIS DEBATES WITH THE LEADERS (20:1—21:38)

It would be obvious at the trials of Jesus that the leaders did not have a solid case against Jesus. They attempted, therefore, to ask Him questions or put Him in difficult situations in order to catch Him saying something offensive or heretical. If they could catch Him in a misstatement, they could use it against Him. When He appeared in public in the Temple on Tuesday of the final week, they seized this opportunity to ask Him some difficult questions. However, when all the questioning and debating was over, it was the religious leaders and not Jesus, who were humbled.

1. The question of authority (20:1-19). Religious authority in Israel was to be found ultimately in the Great Sanhedrin. These men, with Roman permission, were the dominant religious power in the land. Representatives of the Great Sanhedrin questioned Jesus as to where He got His authority for doing "these things" (20:2). "These things" most likely referred to the triumphal entry and the cleansing of the Temple. "These things" would be considered under the jurisdiction of the Great Sanhedrin.

The Lord Jesus answered them with a question that put them in an unescapable dilemma. His question had to do with authority also. He asked them, "Where did John the Baptist get his authority?" They huddled together, concerned not about the truth of the matter but concerned only with how they should answer. If they said his authority was from men (a self-styled prophet), then they faced the wrath of the crowds (20:6). On the other hand, if they said his authority came from God, then they could legitimately be charged with disobedience to God, since they had refused to follow John. Furthermore, they would have been obligated to follow Jesus since John was simply the announcer of Jesus. As a result the leaders had to plead ignorance. They said that they did not know where his authority came from (20:7). Jesus responded to this statement by refusing to answer their question. If these leaders would not acknowledge that John's authority came from God, then it was clear that they certainly would not acknowledge that His came from God. It was useless to make such a claim to these unbelievers.

After their refusal to answer the Lord's question, He launched into a parable that revealed the true spiritual situation in Israel. In this parable the vineyard represents the nation of Israel (so used in the Old Testament of Israel as in Isaiah 5). The tenant farmers in the story represent the leaders of Israel. The owner of the vineyard is God, and the son of the owner is Christ. The servants of the owner represent the prophets of God. Israel had many prophets sent to her, but the leaders of Israel persecuted them and often killed them. Finally, God sent His own Son to them, but they would murder Him too. Therefore, the owner (God) will come and destroy the tenant farmers (Israel's leaders) and give the vineyard to others.

The leaders understood the meaning of the parable, that it was directed toward them (20:19). However, they were unable to move against Jesus because they feared the angry response of the crowd. Their judgment was not far away.

2. The question of paying taxes (20:20-26). A constant source of irritation to the Jews was Roman taxation. Taxation was the indisputable sign that they were under the domination of a Gentile power. The Jews for many years staggered under the weight of the burdensome taxes placed on them by Rome. The patriotic Jews were constantly debating the matter. Later, during the seige of Jerusalem in A.D. 70 by the Romans, it was said that the refusal to pay taxes played a large part in that war. It was a volatile question, therefore, that was asked Jesus by some of His enemies (20:20-22). These verses clearly show that the intention of the Jews was to gather evidence against Christ. Matthew 22:16 reveals that those who came to Jesus with the question "Is it lawful to pay taxes to Caesar?" were sent from the Pharisees and the Herodians (see "Additional Note" on the *Herodians* at the end of the chapter).

Jesus answered their question by asking His questioners whose image was on the coin. They responded by identifying the face on the coin as Caesar's. Jesus then told them to "render to Caesar the things that are Caesar's, and to God the things that are God's" (20:25). The common people and the scholars were both impressed with this answer. God was given His rightful place of supremacy, yet Jesus did not speak against Roman taxation, recognizing that government was ordained of God (see also Romans 13:1-7). It is interesting to note, however, that several days later at His Roman trials, Jesus was accused of forbidding to give tribute to Caesar (Luke 23:2).

3. The question about resurrection (20:27-40). Next came the Sadducees with what was evidently one of their stock questions. (See "Additional Note" on the *Sadducees* at the end of the chapter.) They were attempting to make belief in the resurrection look foolish, and thus make the Lord Himself (who believed in it) to look foolish also. They told a story of a woman who married a man who happened to have six brothers. The man died, and she married one of his brothers. He too died, and she married another brother. In the story the woman eventually marries all seven of these men. The question was, which brother would have her as a wife in the resurrection, since they were all legitimately married to her on earth (20:33)? The story was based on the concept of levirate marriage (Deut. 25:5). Levirate marriage was a means to keep a man's name (and family and inheritance) from dying out if he died childless. His brother could marry his widow, and any children born were credited to the deceased brother.

The Lord responded to this hypothetical question by pointing out two facts. First, life in the resurrection is not a continuation of life as it is lived on the earth (20:34-36). Marriage and the bearing of children will not be part of life in the eternal state. Second, the Lord Jesus addressed the issue of the validity of the concept of resurrection. He pointed out that God is the

God of the living and not of the dead (20:38). He gave proof for this by noting the tense of a verb. He said that at the burning bush (Ex. 3), Moses said that God was, at that moment, Abraham's God and Isaac's God and Jacob's God. Though these three patriarchs had died centuries before, they were alive at that moment. There was an afterlife, and God at that moment was their God. The scribes understood the force of this and agreed that Jesus' use of the Scriptures was valid. They were glad to see the Sadducees silenced.

4. The question about Messiah's lineage (20:41-44). Jesus then took His turn and asked a question. He asked how the Messiah could be of the line of King David and yet be seen as deity? How could Messiah be both God and man? The scholars could understand that Messiah was of David's physical line (see Matt. 22:42), but they simply could not bring together the two ideas of Messiah's humanity and deity. They were baffled and retreated from the debate (see Matt. 22:46).

5. The denunciation of the religious leaders (20:45-47). Once again the Lord denounced the externalism and hypocrisy that was such a dominant characteristic of these men. He warned His own disciples that they should be very wary of these men. These leaders were headed for great judgment.

6. Jesus' observation about giving (21:1-4). After the Lord's opponents left Him, there was for the moment a little calm. As the Lord looked up He observed people putting money in the Temple offering. The Temple treasury consisted of thirteen trumpet-mouthed boxes which stood in the Temple area. Each box had a purpose for which the money placed in it was to be used. Being in a public area, one could make quite a display of one's giving. On this occasion a widow (widows were generally extremely poor) placed two small copper coins in a box. Jesus observed that this widow outgave all the wealthy who were placing large sums in the treasury. The widow has become one of the great New Testament examples of sacrificial giving.

7. *Jesus' prophetic discourse (21:5-38).* Since Jesus had spoken about coming judgment and other events that lay off in the future, His disciples were motivated to ask Him some questions about prophetic events. This section of Luke's gospel is paralleled by Matthew and Mark. When these gospels are compared, a complete record of this prophetic discourse is found (Matt. 24, 25; Mark 13:1-37).

As the disciples and Jesus left the Temple, Jesus told them that the day was coming when the Temple would be completely destroyed (21:6). Four of the disciples (Mark 13:3) asked several questions in light of His declaration. These questions can be reduced to two basic questions: (1) what will signal the destruction of the Temple and Jerusalem, and (2) what are the signs of the second coming? Luke deals more with Christ's answer to the first question, whereas Matthew deals extensively with the answer to the second.

Looking ahead to the time of great tribulation on the earth at the end of the age, the Lord Jesus spoke of the coming judgments that will characterize the first part of that period (21:8-11). (Matt. 24:4-8 along with Rev. 6:1-17 parallels this section of Luke). All three of the synoptics record this material. But the focus in Luke's gospel shifts at 21:12 to deal with the first of the disciples' questions about the Temple. What follows (21:12-24) is a discussion of the apostolic and church age, not the period of the tribulation.

> It is precisely at this point in our Lord's discourse, however, that Luke records a section which has no exact parallel in the other two Gospels. It is, in fact, a literary parenthesis inserted in Luke's account of coming events. This parenthetical section begins with the words, "*But before all these things*" (21:12, ASV), i.e., the things already referred to which will mark the beginning of the "end." The section ends with the words, "*And Jerusalem shall be trodden down of the Gentiles, until the times of the Gentiles be fulfilled*" (21:24). It should be obvious that in this section of Luke's account we have

> the answer of Christ to the disciples' question about the judgment of Jerusalem and the temple for here He speaks especially of the events which will occupy the time from His departure to the destruction of the city in A.D. 70."[2]

Jesus told the disciples that difficult times faced them and other followers of His (21:12-17). Persecution would become part of their lives. This persecution would be the beginning of the signs being foretold by Christ. It is interesting to note that Luke, in writing the book of Acts, records these very things taking place and even uses much of the same language (as in Acts 4:1-3). But this persecution is not to be confused with the times of great judgment in the Tribulation period. In this parenthetical section Luke does not use tribulation terminology, such as the "abomination of desolation" and "great tribulation" (Matt. 24:15, 21). Jesus then warned His hearers that when Jerusalem is surrounded by armies then they are to flee (21:20). This was sound advice for A.D. 70. And although there is similarity of language with the events of the Tribulation (as in Matthew), there is a difference in subject matter.

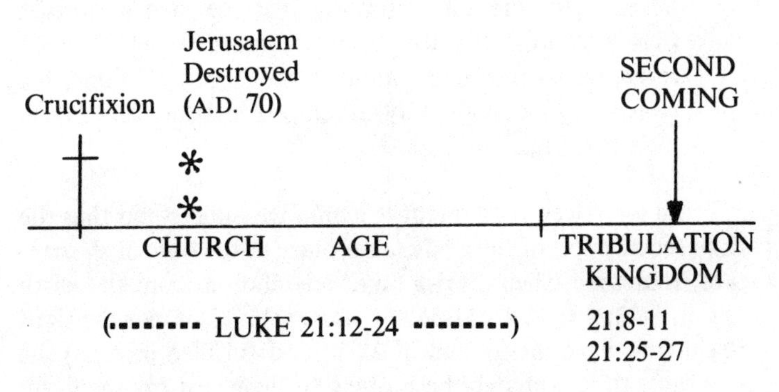

Fig. 4.2

2. Alva J. McClain, *The Greatness of the Kingdom* (Chicago: Moody, 1968), p. 364.

After ending the parenthetical section with a statement about the domination of the Gentiles over Israel (21:24), the Lord Jesus returned to the subject of the end of the age. He spoke of the powerful signs in nature that would cause men to fear (21:25-26). These signs had been spoken about in the Old Testament (Isa. 13:10; Ezek. 32:7; Joel 2:10, 31) and would be once again by John in the book of Revelation (Rev. 6:12-17; 16:8). He also spoke of His glorious second coming to earth (21:27). Only Luke recorded the next statement of the Lord that when these signs begin to take place (as they would in the persecutions of the early church in Acts) then the believer can legitmately look forward to his "redemption drawing near" (21:28).

> Now the "redemption" of Luke 21:28 is not a synonym for the "kingdom of God," but refers to a very specific thing in connection with individual salvation. The Greek term is *apolutrosis* which occurs ten times in the New Testament; and, with the exception of Hebrews 11:35; always refers to personal Christian redemption. . . . Now the "redemption" of Luke 21:28 cannot refer to the salvation of the soul from sin, for the men addressed were certainly already saved. It must therefore be a reference to the redemption of the "body," a doctrine which will be more fully developed in later New Testament writings."[3]

From later New Testament teaching we understand that the final redemption of the body takes place at the time of the rapture, that time when Christ takes His church from the earth (Rom. 8:23; 1 Cor. 15:51-53; 1 Thess. 4:13-18). Once the signs begin (the signs mentioned in 21:12 and fulfilled in Acts) the believer can legitimately be looking heavenward for the event when his body will be redeemed and his salvation completed experiencially.

3. Ibid., p. 367.

When *all* of the signs mentioned by Jesus are seen (Matt. 24:33), then the kingdom of God is about to arrive (21:31). It is obvious from this verse that there is an aspect to the kingdom of God that has not come into existence yet. Those who see the consummation of the signs will see the kingdom as well, as there will be no delay. But the kingdom will not arrive until all the signs are seen. It is not possible, therefore, that this aspect of the kingdom of God is in existence today. This aspect of the kingdom will be established at the glorious second coming of Christ, when He shall rule and reign on this earth.

Jesus concluded His discourse with a warning to be constantly vigilant and not to assume that these events will be long delayed (21:34-36).

D. HIS BETRAYAL AND ARREST (22:1-54)

1. The betrayal by Judas Iscariot (22:1-6). The Jewish leaders were faced with the difficult problem of what to do about Jesus of Nazareth. On the one hand He had forced the issue to such an extent that they had to act. For their own position and authority's sake they could not let Him continue teaching and gathering followers. But on the other hand to arrest Him (especially at a feast time when tens of thousands of the common people were there) would bring down the wrath of the people. This would bring about the intervention of Rome and the loss of their authority and position (John 11:48). The leaders were, therefore, ecstatic when they were approached by Judas Iscariot with a desire to betray Christ. After Judas met with the leaders and agreed upon a price, Judas looked for an opportunity to turn Jesus over to them. Luke carefully records the active role played by Satan and by the religious leaders of Israel (22:3-4).

2. The last supper of Jesus and the disciples (22:7-38). Jesus had an overwhelming desire to spend His last hours with His disciples eating the Passover meal (22:15).

Peter and John were designated by the Lord as the ones to go

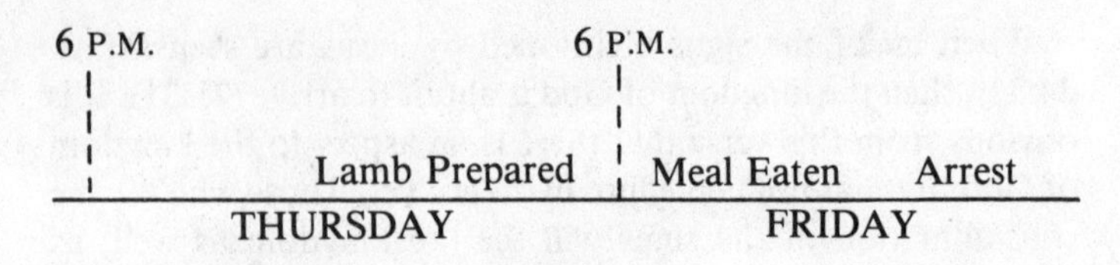

Fig. 4.3

and prepare for the Passover supper. In a rather unusual manner, He gave them directions to the house where they would eat the meal (22:10-12). Jesus obviously knew the location of house, but He also knew that Judas was looking for an opportunity to get Jesus alone so that he could have Him arrested away from the crowds. In order not to be disturbed on this last, very important time with His followers, He gave directions so that Judas could not alert the Jewish leaders as to the location. It would be unusual to see a man carrying water (22:10), as this was the job of women. Peter and John were to follow this clearly designated individual to the place where he went and there prepare for the Passover.

As they gathered to fellowship around the Passover meal, it was clear the Jesus was fully aware of the program of God (22:14-18). He would suffer and die, but that would not be the end. He would be there and fellowship in the coming kingdom. He then instituted the "Lord's Supper." The symbolic, or memorial, nature of the Lord's Supper can be seen here. The phrase "This is My body" (22:19) cannot be taken literally. Obviously it was not His literal body and blood there on the table. He was present bodily quite apart from the elements themselves. Rather He was saying, "This represents My body." The New Covenant based on His blood (22:20) had been prophesied by many in the Old Testament (Isa. 53:1-6; Jer. 31:31). The New Covenant superseded the Old Covenant that came in the days of Moses and is superior to that Old Covenant (2 Cor. 3:5-11).

After instituting the Lord's Supper, Jesus announced that the one who would betray Him was eating supper with Him. It was a part of the divine decree that the death of Christ was to be accompanied by betrayal (22:22). The disciples discussed this betrayal among themselves, uncertain who would do such a thing. It is quite clear from the response of the disciples that Judas Iscariot did not appear any different from the rest of the disciples in his behavior or attitudes.

This discussion about the betrayer evidently sparked the discussion about who would be greatest in the kingdom (22:24). As they thought about who would be so low as to betray the Lord, each disciple began attempting to show why it could not be he and in the process proudly proclaimed his own greatness. It seems amazing from our vantage point that the disciples could behave like this in light of the words of Christ, given moments before, that He must suffer and die. But pride is a very present enemy.

The Lord responded to this discussion by teaching the disciples again that true greatness comes through servanthood. He did promise them that they would indeed have a place in the future kingdom (22:30). The Lord Jesus desired to be with His disciples on this night because, among other reasons, He wanted to instruct them on some important issues. Luke included only a few of His teachings in his gospel, but John 13-16 records many of them and should be read at this point.

The Lord then turned to Peter specifically (perhaps because he was boasting the loudest) and warned that Peter would deny Him (22:31-34). The Lord repeated Peter's name twice for emphasis, thus impressing upon Simon Peter the seriousness of the matter. Satan had requested access to Peter (as to Job), but Christ had prayed on Peter's behalf. Christ prayed that Peter's faith would not become completely shipwrecked when he fell away, but that he would be restored and become an encouragement to the other disciples. Peter, however, informed the Lord that He really did not need to be concerned because his loyalty and steadfastness were limitless. The Lord informed Peter that his limitless loyalty would last about ten hours.

Continuing in the serious vein, the Lord then alerted His men to the fact that persecution was coming (John 15:20), and the atmosphere for ministry would be changed (22:35-38). Before, they went out to the nation of Israel and did not need to take supplies, since the people of the land would support them. No longer would that be true. The environment would become very hostile to them.

3. The agony of Jesus in Gethsemane (22:39-46). The experience of the Lord Jesus in the Garden of Gethsemane reveals much of His humanity and the personal agony that He faced and suffered. The hours in that garden reveal that this time in Christ's life was no casual matter. Salvation is a free gift, but it is not cheap. And the terrible price tag of our salvation is partly revealed in the personal distress, pain, and inner agony of the Lord in Gethsemane.

The text reveals that Jesus had often gone to Gethsemane (22:39). Judas Iscariot would be aware of that, and when he returned to the upper room with the soldiers and did not find Him (assuming that is what he did), he would have known that the Mount of Olives on which was Gethsemane was the likely spot to find Christ. But before Judas and the mob arrived, the stillness of the garden was broken only by Christ's anguished prayers. He prayed that the cup (symbolic of the cross and the accompanying sufferings) might be removed from Him, as He did not want to drink of it (22:42). But the will of the Father became clear; there was no alternate route around the cross. Understanding that, Jesus submitted Himself to the revealed will of the Father and with courage and determination faced the cross and the hours of suffering.

Only Luke reveals that in Gethsemane an angel appeared to Jesus, strengthening Him, and only Luke adds that Jesus' praying was so intense that He sweat, as it were, great drops of blood.

4. The arrest of Jesus in Gethsemane (22:47-53). The Lord had faced and submitted to the will of the Father, and now in the face of His satanically inspired enemies He was fearless and calm. Judas Iscariot led the small army into the garden, and one can only imagine the shock of the disciples as it dawned on them that Judas was the traitor. (All of the gospels emphasize the treachery of Judas by noting that he was "one of the twelve.") When the disciples realized what was happening they asked if they should give armed resistance. Before Jesus answered, one of the disciples (Peter, according to John 18:10) took out his sword and thrust at a man, cutting off his ear. Jesus called a halt to such actions and healed the ear. In spite of this miracle worked in their midst, the enemies of Christ continued on with the arrest. Their treachery is revealed in Jesus' statement that He was with them publicly in the Temple and they did not attempt to arrest Him then. Jesus recognized that the forces of evil were having their day (22:53).

E. HIS TRIALS (22:54—23:25)

1. His trials before the Jews (22:54-71). Before He would finally be placed on the cross, Jesus would go through six trials, three before the Jews and three before the Romans. Luke does not include the first trial before Annas (only John does) but does mention the other five. These trials were, of course, mockeries of true justice and should never have taken place.

The first trial recorded by Luke (Christ's second trial) was before the high priest Caiaphas (22:54, 63-65). Here Jesus endured much mockery, physical abuse, and false accusations. This trial, which was illegal (since it had been less than 24 hours since His arrest and since it was still in the hours of darkness—both of which violated Jewish law), was inconclusive and thus He was brought before the Great Sanhedrin at daybreak (22:66). In the midst of the account of the trials, Luke included the denials of Peter (22:54-62). The very thing that Peter vehemently denied that he would do, he did. And not just once, but three times, he forcefully claimed that he did not even know Jesus Christ, much less was one of His followers. The crowing of the cock brought Peter back to his senses. He realized how he had miserably failed, and he wept bitterly (22:62). But Jesus had prayed for Peter's restoration (22:32) and later would personally forgive and restore the fallen Peter (24:34).

The trial before the Great Sanhedrin was a crucial one since this was the most powerful religious and legal body in Israel. They immediately questioned Him on His messianic claims. Jesus understood that they were set in their unbelief, but He also realized that these men were in the place of God-given authority. (Jesus had said they were to be obeyed since they sat in the seat of Moses, Matt. 23:2-3). After speaking of their unbelief, the Lord Jesus did claim to be Messiah, the Son of Man (a phrase out of Daniel 7). They then asked Him if He was the Son of God, and Jesus responded in the affirmative (22:70). Their response was one of angry enthusiasm. They no longer needed to seek for witnesses against Jesus as they themselves had heard His claims and now became witnesses against Him.

2. His trials before the Romans (23:1-25). The Sanhedrin members realized that since they had been stripped of the power of capital punishment, they would have to go to the Roman officials to seek the death penalty for Jesus. They also realized that a charge of blasphemy would have little weight with Rome. So it became necessary to alter the charges against Him and make them political in nature. Treason, rebellion, and such matters were of great interest to Rome, but not violations of religious law. So certain charges of a political nature were leveled against Jesus before the Roman governor, Pilate (23:1-2, 5).

Pilate questioned Jesus, and Jesus (in John's gospel) answered the charge of His kingship. Pilate became convinced that this Jesus was just a religious enthusiast and was rather harmless. Pilate understood that the charges were trumped up by the Jews because of their hatred of Jesus (Matt. 27:18). He was irritated with the Jewish leaders at this point, but later that irritation would turn to fear as the whole ugly scene began to unfold (John 19:8). It is interesting to note the role of the leaders in these trials (23:2, 5, 10, 18, 21, 23).

Since Jesus was from Galilee, which was Herod's district, and since Herod was in Jerusalem attending the feast, Pilate decided to get out of the situation by sending Jesus to Herod (23:6-12). Herod, who had wanted to see Jesus for some time, was glad to have this opportunity to meet Him. Herod questioned Him, mocked Him, and treated Him with contempt. Jesus never said one word. He had nothing to say to Herod, since Herod had not listened to the forerunner, John the Baptist. Herod, after hearing all the accusations against Jesus (23:10), did nothing but send Jesus back to Pilate.

Luke notes that this event did help the relationship between Pilate and Herod (23:12). The cause of previous enmity between them was probably some question of jurisdiction. To Herod this event was interpreted as Pilate's recognition of Herod's jurisdiction and authority.

Once again Jesus was brought before Pilate (23:13-25). Pilate tried to release Him. Why would a Roman official who had killed hundreds of Jews try to preserve one Jewish "peasant"? There were probably several factors that motivated Pilate. First, his wife had a dream, and she warned Pilate to stay away from Jesus (Matt. 27:19). Second, Jesus claimed to be the Son of God and, being a Roman who believed that gods did come and live among men, Pilate was afraid of dealing with such an individual (John 19:7-8). Third, the calm but powerful personality of Jesus impressed Pilate in the trials. And fourth, Pilate was also motivated by his hatred for these religious leaders, who were constantly giving him trouble. Luke records Pilate's declarations of not guilty several times (23:4, 14, 15, 22). He tried several schemes to pacify the Jews and get Jesus released, but to no avail. Eventually Pilate caved in under the pressure of the situation and turned over Jesus to the religious leaders in order to put Him to death (23:25).

F. His Death (23:26-56)

1. On the way to the crucifixion (23:26-32). During His trials the Lord Jesus had suffered much physical abuse. He had been struck, beaten, and scourged. Scourging alone has been known to kill a man, and it is therefore understandable that someone else had to actually carry the cross for the weakened Jesus (23:26). A number of people were deeply grieved over what was happening and wept. But Jesus turned to them and told them not to weep for Him but for the Jewish nation (23:28). Days of terrible judgment were going to descend on Israel because of their rejection of their own Messiah. Jesus concluded His warning to those who were mourning for Him by uttering a proverbial saying (23:31). The saying probably means that if the Romans beat and kill one that they acknowledge to be innocent (Jesus = the green tree), then imagine what they will do to those who are guilty (Israel = the dry tree).

Luke also takes note that two others would be involved in the execution that day (23:32). Those two were both convicted criminals.

2. The crucifixion of Jesus (23:33-49). Jesus was led, along with the two criminals, to the Place of the Skull (23:33). Calvary, as it is commonly known, may have been the common site of execution located north of the city wall in an old rock quarry. It is possible that the "skull rock" still visible today was the backdrop for many Roman executions, including that of the Lord Jesus. (It should be noted that no gospel writer says that Jesus was put to death on top of a hill, though many hymns do say that.)

The gospel writers do not go into great detail about the crucifixion event itself. They simply state that Jesus was crucified, knowing full well the terrible physical pain that He endured.

While on the cross, Jesus uttered seven sayings. Luke records three of these sayigs: the first, the second, and the seventh. The first saying, "Father forgive them; for they do not know what they are doing," was a cry that revealed the merciful nature of the Lord Jesus. The words "forgive them" have the idea of "letting them go." Jesus was not praying that their sins would be cleansed (they would have to pray that for themselves), but rather that the Father would not at that moment destroy them for this greatest of all sins, crucifying the Son of God. God had struck men down in the past for tampering with that which was sacred, and these men certainly faced that kind of judgment. But God answered that prayer, and those who crucified Him were given time to repent.

Even while Jesus was on the cross, the Jews mocked Him, revealing their satanic hatred for Him (23:35). And the two thieves joined in the mockery (23:39). One of the criminals, in desperation, hoped that Jesus would work a miracle and get them all out of the predicament they were in. His words were saturated in bitterness, however, and what came out was more of a taunt than a request. The second man could not save his life but could save his soul. His statement concerning Jesus' coming into His kingdom is a statement of genuine faith (23:42), and to that faith Jesus responded. Jesus encouraged this thief with, "Today you shall be with Me in Paradise" (this is the second saying of Jesus). At death, Jesus' body was placed in the tomb, but His immaterial part (soul/spirit) went to be with the Father.* When the thief died, he too eventually went to be with the Father and shared the afterlife with the Lord Jesus.

Several supernatural things occurred in connection with the crucifixion, and Luke records two of these: (1) the supernatural darkness in the middle of the day from noon to 3:00 P.M. and (2) the tearing of the thick veil in the Temple (23:44-45). The darkness symbolized the spiritual blackness of that moment as the perfect Lamb of God became sin for us, and upon that scene no one could look. The tearing of the veil symbolized the opening of access to God that was made possible by the death of Christ (Heb. 9:3, 8; 10:19-20).

When Jesus had finished paying the incredible debt of sin, He dismissed His spirit and said, "Father, into Thy hands I

* Some Bible scholars believe that Jesus did not go to the Father until His resurrection, emptying paradise, which is seen as the abode of the righteous dead. Others view paradise as simply an equivalent to heaven. In either case, the repentant thief was given a marvelous, comforting promise by Christ.

commit My spirit'' (the seventh saying from the cross).

The reaction of the onlookers was that of grief, awe, and anguish. They sensed that something awful had happened. And they were right, if He stayed dead.

3. The burial of Jesus (23:50-56). In his foundation truths of the gospel, the apostle Paul included the burial of Christ (1 Cor. 15:3-4). The burial was objective proof that Jesus did indeed die on the cross.

One of the members of the Great Sanhedrin, Joseph, came and requested the body of Christ from Pilate. He, of course, would have had no part in the condemning of Christ, as he evidently was a secret follower (John 12:42). He could remain secret no longer, however, and be part to this horrible crime of murder. With new boldness, along with Nicodemus (John 19:39), he placed the body of Jesus into his own tomb. Some of the women who had followed Jesus took note of the burial spot and went home to prepare spices so that they could finish preparing the body on Sunday, the day after the Sabbath (23:54-56).

Additional Notes

THE HERODIANS

The Herodians were more of a political party than a religious sect. They were Jewish supporters of the Herodian dynasty. They were desirous of the political power and worldly benefits that came to loyal supporters of Herods' family. Normally the Herodians and the Pharisees were archenemies. But in the case of Christ they temporarily set aside their antagonism in order to unite against a common enemy.

THE SADDUCEES

The sect of the Sadducees originated during the intertestament period in reaction to the merging party of the Pharisees. The name *sadducee* may have been derived from Zadok, who was the high priest in the days of David and Solomon. Another possibility is that the name might have come from the word *zedekah* which means "righteousness."

Since most of our information about the Sadducees comes from their enemies, there is some uncertainty about certain statements. However, it is clear that they refused to accept the oral law developed by the Pharisees. They seemed to have limited the full authority of Scripture to just the five books of Moses (Genesis-Deuteronomy). They evidently did not believe in angels, demons, resurrection, or a coming Messiah.

They were less numerous than the Pharisees, but they were generally wealthy and in places of authority. The Sadducean party included high-ranking priests and the wealthy lay nobility. Because they had so much prestige, power, and wealth to lose, they were far more cooperative with Rome than were the Pharisees. As a sect, they ceased to exist after the destruction of the city of Jerusalem in A.D. 70.

5

THE FINAL AUTHENTICATION OF JESUS THE SON OF MAN

(LUKE 24:1-53)

A. HIS EMPTY TOMB (24:1-12)

There can be no doubt that the resurrection of Jesus Christ permeates the entire New Testament and is the foundation on which the Christian faith is built. No resurrection means no Christian faith (1 Cor. 15:12-20). Perhaps one of the greatest evidences of the resurrection is seen in this chapter of Luke—the radical change that occurred in the lives of the disciples who went from depression to joy and from fear to boldness. Besides this, several resurrection appearances are recorded in this final chapter of Luke.

The women who came to the tomb that Sunday morning had love, but they had no hope. They came with their spices for the body of Jesus but were afraid that they would not even be able to get at the body because of the heavy stone (Mark 16:3). When they arrived at the tomb the stone was already rolled away from the entrance. Though the body was gone and the tomb was empty, they did not believe that He was alive. Undoubtedly a variety of explanations were discussed. Suddenly two men appeared (undoubtedly angels) and informed them that Jesus was alive (24:6-7). The women were reminded that Jesus had often spoken of His rising from the dead. (Luke records several of those times: 9:22; 18:32-33). The women did what they should have done—they told the men who had been selected by Christ as His apostles. Unfortunately, these men did not respond in faith either. Peter did go and (with John) investigate and was amazed by what he saw.

THE RESURRECTION APPEARANCES OF CHRIST

RESURRECTION APPEARANCES	PLACE	TIME	LUKE	OTHER SCRIPTURES
To Mary Magdalene	Jerusalem	Sunday	___	JOHN, MARK
To Some Other Women	Jerusalem	Sunday	___	MATTHEW
To Peter	Jerusalem	Sunday	24:34	1 CORINTHIANS
To Emmaus Disciples	Emmaus	Sunday	24:13	MARK
To 10 Disciples	Jerusalem	Sunday	24:36	JOHN
To 11 Disciples	Jerusalem	A week later	___	JOHN, 1 COR.
To 7 Disciples	Galilee	?	___	JOHN
To 500 at one time	?	?	___	1 CORINTHIANS
To James (Jesus brother)	?	?	___	1 CORINTHIANS
To the Eleven	Galilee	?	___	MATTHEW, MARK
To the Eleven	Jerusalem	40 days later	24:44	ACTS

Fig. 5.1

B. HIS EMMAUS DISCIPLES (24:13-35)

On that same Sunday two followers of Christ were returning from the Passover celebration to their home at Emmaus, some seven miles from Jerusalem. Jesus joined Cleopas (24:18) and his companion, but they did not recognize Him. They related to Him the recently transpired events and their personal disappointment in what had happened (24:18-21). They even mentioned the empty tomb. But the knowledge of the tomb's being empty did not produce faith in them any more than it had in the women. Jesus mildly rebuked them (24:25) and went on to explain the Old Testament Scriptures to them, emphasizing the sufferings of Messiah.

They invited Jesus to join them for supper and continued their course in Old Testament survey. As He broke the bread (unusual since He was not the host), they recognized Him. Did they see the nail prints for the first time? Did they recognize His manner of breaking bread and giving thanks? Perhaps both, coupled with the fact that God opened their eyes to really see Him. When they came to understand the Scriptures, they saw Him as never before.

Jesus disappeared, and the Emmaus disciples hurried the seven miles back to Jerusalem to inform the apostles that Jesus was actually alive. When they got there, they were informed that Simon Peter had seen the Lord also.

C. HIS RESURRECTION APPEARANCES (24:36-49)

The sharing of experiences was interrupted by the sudden and unusual appearance of Christ (24:36). Their fright soon turned to joy as the ten disciples plus the two from Emmaus came to realize that He had come back from the grave. His body was the same, yet it was different. He could be touched because He had flesh and bones (24:39), and He could eat food (24:42-43), yet He was able to appear and disappear.

About one month later Jesus gave them further instruction about Himself and about their responsibility to be witnesses for Him (24:44-48). Luke does not note the time distinction, but by comparison with parallel passages it is clear that there is actually a break in time between verses 43 and 44. In His instructions, Jesus told them that they were to remain in Jerusalem until the promised Holy Spirit would come (see John 14:26; 15:26; and 16:7-15 where the promise is made). Luke in his book of Acts will record the fulfillment of this promise (Acts 2:1-4).

D. HIS ASCENSION INTO HEAVEN 24:50-53

The Lord's earthly ministry was over. He had lived a pure, sinless life. He had done the preaching, teaching, and miracle working that needed to be done. He had died for the sin of all mankind, and He had victoriously come back from the tomb. He had prepared a group of followers to carry on the work He began and to begin a new work (the church). Now the Lord God, who had taken on the form of a man and was born of a virgin over thirty years before, was now returning to His rightful glory with the Father. His followers could not help but praise and worship Him.

Luke began and ended his gospel in the Temple, but what a change had taken place. The old covenant had been set aside, and the new covenant with all its hope, power, and reality had been established.

SELECTED BIBLIOGRAPHY

Bailey, Kenneth E. *Poet and Peasant and Through Peasant Eyes.* Grand Rapids: Eerdmans, 1982.

Edersheim, Alfred. *Sketches of Jewish Social Life in the Days of Christ.* Grand Rapids: Eerdmans, 1967.

Edersheim, Alfred. *The Life and Times of Jesus the Messiah.* 2 vols. New York: Longmans, Green, 1900.

Geldenhuys, Norval. *Commentary on the Gospel of Luke.* Grand Rapids: Eerdmans, 1966.

Hoehner, Harold W. *Chronological Aspects of the Life of Christ.* Grand Rapids: Zondervan, 1978.

______. *Herod Antipas.* Grand Rapids: Zondervan, 1980.

Jeremias, Joachim, *Jerusalem in the Time of Jesus.* Philadelphia: Fortress, 1969.

McClain, Alva J. *The Greatness of the Kingdom.* Chicago: Moody, 1968.

Morris, Leon. *The Gospel According to St. Luke.* Grand Rapids: Eerdmans, 1982.

Plummer, Alfred. *A Critical and Exegetical Commentary on the Gospel According to St. Luke.* 3d ed. Edinburgh: T. and T. Clark, 1900.

Pentecost, J. D. *Things to Come.* Grand Rapids: Dunham, 1964.

Schurer, Emil. *A History of the Jewish People in the Time of Jesus.* New York: Schocken, 1961.

Scroggie, W. Graham, *A Guide to the Gospels.* Old Tappan, N. J.: Revell, 1962.

Thomas, Robert L., and Gundry, Stanley N. *A Harmony of the Gospels.* Chicago: Moody, 1978.

Moody Press, a ministry of the Moody Bible Institute, is designed for education, evangelization, and edification. If we may assist you in knowing more about Christ and the Christian life, please write us without obligation: Moody Press, c/o MLM, Chicago, Illinois 60610.

NOTES

NOTES

NOTES

NOTES

NOTES

NOTES

NOTES

NOTES

NOTES

NOTES